UNCAGED
The biography of
NICOLAS CAGE

Douglas Thompson

BOXTREE

for Domino

First published in 1997 by Boxtree

an imprint of Macmillan Publishers Ltd
25 Eccleston Place, London SW1W 9NF
and Basingstoke

Associated companies throughout the world

ISBN: 07522 1190 0

1 2 3 4 5 6 7 8 9 10

A CIP catalogue entry for this book is available from the British Library.

Designed by Nigel Davies

Printed and bound in Great Britain by Mackays of Chatham plc, Chatham, Kent

Contents

Acknowledgments

My thanks to the many people who have helped me put the madcap life of Nicolas Cage into perspective. Most of all thanks to Cage for his time, and for being so talented to merit, at an early age, a thorough examination of his professional and private life. My gratitude to Charlie Carman at Boxtree for the chance to do so and, as always, extra special thanks to literary agent Judith Chilcote.

Prologue

Look Back in Awe

'I needed to get back to that angry, young audience.' Nicolas Cage, on making *Vampire's Kiss* in 1989

When he was twelve years old and first asked to perform in public by an internationally renowned, Oscar-winning director, Nicolas Coppola was a confident little brat.

Francis Ford Coppola was trying to impress some Japanese visitors at his rambling country home in northern California. These were Tokyo moneymen, potential investors in his 1976 movie plans, and he wanted to show that he cared for them as well as their yen. What better than that his nephew Nicolas should talk to them in their own language? 'You know,' says the nephew, now officially Nicolas Cage and recalling the incident a few months before his thirty-third birthday on 7 January 1997, 'it was, like, a big moment that one of the family was going to say something in Japanese to this Japanese businessman. So I looked at him and I said "*Yasai*." The Japanese guy says: "That's great. You know, most people say hello or good evening. No one's ever said, 'Vegetable,' to me when we met."'

Flash forward to 1990 and Nicolas Cage, admired rebel and Hollywood star, is attending the Cannes Film Festival with his film *Wild at Heart* and the controversial director David Lynch, who had become a household name through his offbeat but mainstream television series *Twin Peaks*. Yet again, a famous director was asking the unprepared Cage to do something special.

He believed he'd finished being a ghost of Elvis in the film in which, as the memorable Sailor Ripley, he completed a randy, super-sexually-charged couple with co-star Laura Dern. 'I was taking the biggest American icon, Elvis Presley, and trying to do an impersonation. You know how Andy Warhol would take these fantastic icons like Muhammad Ali or Marilyn Monroe and do that with them? I was going to try and do that with acting. David Lynch, being such an intense Presley fan, saw it as an opportunity to get as close to casting his hero as he was ever going to get. This was the kind of movie I wish Presley had made. For me it was horrifying to sing two Elvis songs in *Wild at Heart.* When you have one of the greatest directors in the world telling you that you're gonna do a couple of Elvis numbers and what's more you're going to sound *just like Elvis* that's a lot of pressure. Thank God, they souped up my voice a little.

'Then at Cannes there was a big banquet with 400 people all dressed up to the nines in tuxes and evening gowns. I was sitting there with David and Laura Dern and the president of the festival and his wife, and the president's wife said: "Would you please sing 'Love Me Tender' for me?" I just went *white* and started trembling. David wanted me to do it. He was like: "Nicster, buddy, man, ya jump up on the table and ya sing to her, *now!*" There was no backing out. So, I did jump up on the table and in this quavering, eggshell voice sang "Love Me Tender" to her with sweat drenching my forehead. Then I got down and was met with fairly courteous applause – though obviously it was courtesy applause. But it had to be done. So I did it. It was one of the most terrifying things I've ever had to do and probably the most embarrassing.'

Cage has worked with great names and great characters in twenty-six films, from Sean Penn to Sean Young to Sean Connery, and has developed intense relationships with his co-stars and with the constantly developing and changing Hollywood. His story is their story and vice versa.

He is the master of quirky roles that walk a not always straight line between sanity and dementia. He's put on quite a mad act off screen too. A 1996 Oscar winner for *Leaving Las Vegas* and a box-office champion that same year for *The Rock*, he had an even higher profile in 1997 with the disaster-in-the-skies flying penitentiary movie *Con Air*, co-starring with John Malkovich and John Cusack, and the futuristic action thriller *Face Off*, in which he co-starred with that other high-flying performer of the late 1990s, John Travolta.

The combination of his Oscar and his 1997 raft of films catapulted him up the year's annual 'Most Powerful People in Hollywood' list. He went from nowhere to number 73 beating Sean Connery, Eddie Murphy, Sylvester Stallone and George Clooney in a line-up dominated by behind-the-scenes producers and directors. For on-screen talent to rate on the list at all is considered a giant achievement. The compilers noted that his ranking was endorsed by him being Warner Brothers first choice for the title role of *Superman Reborn*.

The actor with the big moon eyes and dark, almost malevolent image talks slowly as he reflects on his life. It could, he says, have been so different. Of his early days he says: 'I was charged with a great deal of anger, a well of passion, and I really wanted to get it out. I had an edge. I had a temper – I could do things very spontaneously. If it wasn't for acting I probably wouldn't have been able to channel it. I would probably be in jail. I guess I should be careful what I say but I have at times had criminal tendencies.'

A decade ago Cage played Cher's lover in *Moonstruck*. She won an Oscar and he earned respect as the one-handed baker she can't resist. He says that then he was borrowing gestures from silent movies.

'If you look at *Metropolis* (the futuristic fantasy made by Fritz Lang in 1926) there's a shot of the scientist who invents the technology to create the robot woman – he shows off the robot hand that he invented. He has it raised up. I told Norman Jewison, who was directing *Moonstruck*, that I really wanted to approximate that shot. He thought it was nuts but he went for it – so I could pull the glove off and show the wooden hand.'

The film established Cage as a romantic leading man and as an actor who could be indulged (to good effect) by directors as powerful and talented as Jewison, who called Cage 'a poet who will do anything'.

Certainly, the success of *Moonstruck* spooked Cage: 'I'd always been playing to a different audience, a more rebellious, angry, young audience. *Moonstruck* was older than I was in some ways. Now I look at it and think it's a beautiful movie but then I revolted and did *Vampire's Kiss* because I needed to get back to that angry, young audience.'

As the New York yuppie who becomes a vampire, Cage's performance in *Vampire's Kiss* is perhaps his best known if, ironically, the film is one of his least successful cinema releases. When it opened in 1989 it did not do well critically or commercially. Nearly a decade on, its video life looks endless – it's the movie in which he ate a live cockroach.

'To this day, people ask me about that fucking cockroach – it was disgusting! I actually have a fear of bugs and I had to disinfect my mouth with like, 100%-proof vodka and just spit the bug out. It makes me sick thinking about it. But just eating that bug created a miniature shock wave. I thought if Pete Townsend could smash his guitar with The Who then I could damn well eat the bug. I reckon it saved some serious money in special effects.

'I really ate that live cockroach. The script said it was supposed to be a raw egg but it didn't make sense to me that the character would eat a raw egg. He thinks he's a vampire. I was trying to graduate up the food chain from pistachio to cockroach to pigeon to person. It was logical. It couldn't be a fake cockroach. It had to be real. I wanted everyone to know that bug went into my mouth. I knew if I ate the bug we would still be talking about the movie today.

'The fact is, I'm not sure I like being associated with cockroaches. I'm not that wild about them. Yet cockroaches and I have become linked. My manager threw a birthday party for me once and there was a giant cake in the shape of a fucking cockroach. But, yes, I ate the bug and and when you go to the theatre it's the same reaction – *oh, no!* It had to be done. So I did it.'

Chapter One
Between The Rock and an Oscar

'The Oscar took care of all the past hurts – it told me I wasn't crazy.'

Nicolas Cage, 1996

D uring the warm mid-afternoon of 25 March 1996, in southern California, Nicolas Cage somehow *knew* he was going to be named Best Actor at the sixty-eighth annual Academy Awards. His performance as a suicidal alcoholic in *Leaving Las Vegas* had gathered a string of American and international awards and accolades, including the Golden Globe – and this despite the movie being, like its star, a maverick in the Hollywood mainstream. Made on a tiny budget by British director Mike Figgis, this was the film Cage's advisers – even his friends and family – had told him not to make. It was too dark, too risky.

But to Cage that had simply made the project more intriguing – and Oscar night more exciting. Hollywood's studio system is increasingly ossified and the clearer the focus on independent films – in 1997 movies like *The English Patient, Breaking the Waves* and *Shine* – the brighter the atmosphere seems at the end of the red carpet inside the Dorothy Chandler Pavilion in downtown Los Angeles.

Which was where Nicolas Cage saw himself as he fingered the wide lapel of his Hugo Boss tuxedo. Although he was a favourite for the Best Actor Oscar, he was acutely aware that the competition was strong, especially from that other former Brat Packer Sean Penn, as the condemned man in *Dead Man Walking*. Penn's performance opposite Susan Sarandon had staunch support from voters.

Sir Anthony Hopkins, an Oscar winner for *Silence of the Lambs*, was in the running for the title role in director Oliver Stone's *Nixon*. Richard Dreyfuss, a winner in 1978 for *The Goodbye Girl*, was back on best form with *Mr Holland's Opus*. The dark horse was Italian actor Massimo Troisi who had died two days after the Oscar nominated *Il Postino* was completed. Cage was the front runner.

As his black stretch limousine approached Spring Street he held on tightly to the hand of his wife Patricia Arquette (they had danced a tango in their penthouse apartment to calm him before leaving for the ceremonies) as they sat listening nervously to the radio broadcasting the cheers of the crowd outside the Dorothy Chandler auditorium. Cage, who did not use the Coppola name to avoid charges of nepotism and indulgence from the Hollywood community, had not written an acceptance speech – he did not want to jinx his chances of winning. He believes you make your own luck and should give it every chance. There were three hours to go before he would really know the result. But he turned and smiled at his wife. He recalled: 'I am very superstitious and I don't know why but seven has always been my lucky number. I was born on the seventh and many of the critics' awards were given out on the seventh. *Leaving Las Vegas* was filmed in 16mm and one and six adds up to seven. You get the picture? I like the number seven. So, I'm looking out the window and I see a street sign on a wall that says in big, red letters: Speed Limit: 7 Miles an Hour. Have you ever heard of a street sign like that in your life? I hadn't. I don't even know what street we were on but I knew that it meant something. I knew that it meant I was going to win. I know that sounds weird but I just knew.'

Weird? No, just Nicolas Cage. Forget the crystal balls and tarot cards. Cage uses street signs. But the reality of either winning (and having to walk up to the podium) or losing (and keeping the frozen smile in place) before a billion television viewers is stressful, no matter how confident you *think* you are: 'I had woken up in a good space and managed to go with it and relax. Though people were using the term "front runner" I'm never one to assume anything. What would happen, I worried, if I got my hopes up and nothing happened because no one had seen the film? It gives you a kind of terrible stage fright when you start thinking. In some ways it was worse that I had been predicted to win. I'm not one to assume. I didn't want to prepare a speech. I'd written one in case I won the Independent Spirit Award that was presented a few weeks earlier. When Sean Penn won that one I crumpled up my speech and threw it out. It's not something you want to do to yourself and I was afraid that would happen again. And when it comes down to the eleventh hour you're going to get caught up in the excitement of the moment. You try to relax but then you start thinking about winning and you start thinking about losing.

'And you realize that winning is better than losing.

'Then Jessica Lange opened the envelope and I could hear her utter the letter "N". She hadn't even got the rest of my first name and I knew I was in. Surprisingly, my feet worked OK on the way up to the stage. I think it's because a good friend of mine [actor Jim Carrey] told me not to let the moment pass me by. And I didn't. I took it all in. I even remembered to breathe. It was a damn fine moment.

'The image that sticks – and it's strange – is Jessica Lange wiping my wife's lipstick off my mouth as we rode the elevator up to the press room. That and the wave of calm as she read my name – it's not something that happens every day.

'When you get an Oscar you are being recognized by your peers and that was important to me. The prejudice I experienced because of my name was like a pitchfork in my butt and it made me work twice as hard at everything I did. The Oscar took fifteen years but it took care of all the past hurts.

'But the Oscar had meaning way beyond resolving some pain. It told me I wasn't crazy all these years when I picked the roles I did. The fact that the Academy noticed me was really brave of them. And good for the industry and the future of alternative movies. The award encouraged me to keep following my heart. There had been a reason for what I did and the Oscar said that my ideas weren't wrong. I've always tried to do the unexpected.'

Which he did when he followed his award-winning role as the self-destructive Ben Sanderson in *Leaving Las Vegas* with nerdy hero Stanley Goodspeed opposite Sean Connery in *The Rock*. When Cage took him on, Stanley, an FBI lab specialist who finds himself smack in the middle of gunplay and explosions, became Hollywood's most unexpected hero.

'With the kind of career I've had there was never room for an action picture until then, but if I was going to enter that arena I didn't want to enter it as a robotic, stoic, steroid-chomping, supermacho metal head. That's not me. I wanted to enter it as a human being, a more or less reluctant hero who is not a violent man and who does not want to kill people. I could never have played Stanley as a guy who is working in a lab out of frustration because he really wants to be out in the field killing people. I couldn't have done that with dignity. I told them he had to be a guy who loves being in the lab but is in the field because he's forced to be. He can't help it. He does what he does because it has to be done.'

Cage's family are used to Tinseltown gold: his grandfather, Carmine Coppola, won, with Nino Rota, an Oscar for the Best Original Dramatic Score for *The Godfather: Part II* in 1974, and his uncle, Francis Ford Coppola, was named Best Director for the same film. When Cage clutched his own statuette he exclaimed: 'Oh, boy – a $3.5 million budget, some 16-millimetre stock footage thrown in, and I'm holding one of these!'

In the Hollywood world of movie budgets that soar to more than $100 million, in which special effects have overtaken plot and character, it was an incredible achievement for all involved. And immensely appropriate that Cage, of all actors, was the standard bearer.

But even with hindsight he still remains pragmatic about the circumstances in which he made *Leaving Las Vegas*. His close friend Jim Carrey, an Oscar presenter that night, offered the memorable line to the black tie audience that the Academy Awards are merely 'the lord of all knick knacks', and Cage has been around long enough to recognize that finance will always dictate to some extent which movies get made: 'Some of my films have made money and I'm glad they have. I would never have been able to do *Leaving Las Vegas* if I hadn't had some commercial success before that. If I hadn't had some semblance of a career I never would have had enough money to do that film. Part of my plan has been to constantly change and do the unexpected. And because I've always believed that these unexpected hidden treasures, like *Leaving Las Vegas*, keep coming my way. I never expected people to see the film and I certainly didn't expect to win any awards from it. That was fine with me; that's not why I did it. I did it because it was a great role. I did it because it was different. The amazing thing is that, unbeknownst to me, the country had shifted in attitude and was taking a new look at cinema. People were interested in different things and I wasn't even aware of it. For the first time in my life my tastes were in synch with other people's. How weird is that?'

Chapter Two

Dynasty – Italian Style

'I want to thank my son Francis because without him I wouldn't be here. But then, if I wasn't here, he wouldn't be either.' Carmine Coppola, on accepting his Oscar at the 1975

Academy Award ceremonies

Nicolas Coppola's great-grandfather, Francesco Pennino, arrived in America from Naples in the early 1900s. He played the piano for Enrico Caruso, arguably this century's first opera pop star, who was played by Mario Lanza in the 1951 film *The Great Caruso*. Like the movies, the opera business is about talent *and* temperament. The extremes of both are often condoned as artistic licence.

The boy who became Nicolas Cage was born into a family with an eccentric, flamboyant history, a genetic classroom for a young man destined always to take the most difficult and complicated path. The Coppolas are a vibrant, theatrical clan and although Cage changed his name he could not erase his place in the dynasty; indeed his success has only emphasized it.

Francis Ford Coppola, so named after *his* grandfather and the car which was the symbol of his birthplace, Detroit, became an established movie-maker who created a family film network in employing his parents, sister, children and nephew. His sister Talia Shire – Connie in *The Godfather* saga, Sylvester Stallone's wife in the *Rocky* movies – has pondered often on the wisdom of the clan working together: 'In circus families the most dangerous acts are the ones done by family members because if you're risking your life and there's no net it had better be your brother or your mother who is going to catch you. If I ever do a triple flip as an actress it really won't be with a lot of directors. It would be with my brother Francis because I know that if I go to the limit with my ability he will structure me and edit me to look my best.

'In one sense it's damn dangerous to work with family, you're taking an enormous risk, and in another you'll do your best work. Francis will get the best out of Nicolas as he did out of my father. He'll take me as far as I can go and I know it'll be there on the screen. And by the same token I know I would do the same for him.

'Americans are peculiar about nepotism. We left the British Empire because we didn't like royal families. And that's absolutely right – you do it on your own. At the same time we love it if something tells us a family does have magic and we can see it passed on. It's a peculiar contradiction about royalty.'

The family still argues as to whether Nicolas Cage's gifts come from the Coppola or Pennino side of the family. Carmine Coppola grew up in New York and received a scholarship to the Juilliard Academy where he became friends with another student, a trumpeter called Albert Pennino, who took the young Carmine home to meet his family, which included his sister Italia. His friend instantly fell in love with her and a dynasty was born. Film historian Stephen Farber says that no other latter-day film family has formed such an extensive network of working relationships: 'Not since Universal Studios' founder Carl Laemmle populated his studio with a horde of relatives from Bavaria have so many members of one movieland family worked together so frequently. The novelty in the Coppola family is that the son is the prime mover and shaker, not the father. Francis made it on his own but once he was established he hired his father, brother, sister, nephew and children.'

Italia's father, Francesco, was a popular songwriter as well as a pianist. He also wrote plays and an excerpt from one of them is included in *Godfather II* in a scene with Robert De Niro's young Vito Corleone. Francesco wanted to pursue fame in America and with his family undertook the eleven-week trip by sea from Naples to Ellis Island, New York. It was an unknown land and future for him and his family. In the Great Hall they underwent the medical and legal formalities.

Each immigrant, a manifest tag attached to their coat, was asked thirty questions in two minutes. In English. As they were quizzed, an interpreter stood by.

'What is your name?'

'Are you an anarchist?'

'Do you have a criminal record?'

'Do you have any skills?' Francesco Pennino did. As he was waiting for his interview he was composing his most famous song, 'Goodbye to Naples', in his head. He also established vast contacts in the Italian community in Brooklyn where he settled. He saw the market for entertainment from the Old World and organised the first films to be imported from Italy into America, and during this silent era in Hollywood he was asked to work for Paramount Studios – the company that made *The Godfather* films – but turned them down. His daughter Italia would recall:

'He said he didn't want his children in Hollywood.'

Italia Pennino Coppola was a loyal daughter. She always resented the assumption that her son Francis was the first family member to make it in the movies and that her children's talents came from her husband's family.

'From some of the things Carmine said,' she recalled in 1983, 'you get the impression that if I had married a barber my sons would be a bunch of stupid barbers. But there's more music on *my* side of the family than on his.'

During that discussion her husband interrupted: 'Now I resent what you are saying. Yours was not a musical family. You didn't talk about symphonic music and about opera which I did.'

His wife retorted: 'No my father didn't sit home and talk about opera but he gave us all piano lessons. Music comes from both sides of the family.'

As does the fiery temperament. Of Cage's name change from Coppola's his grandmother said: 'It was a stupid, dumb jerk thing.' From that her grandson considered that she didn't approve.

When he graduated from the Juilliard, Carmine Coppola worked with the Radio City Musical Hall orchestra and his first son, August, was born in 1934. Shortly afterwards the family moved to Detroit when he became first flautist with the Detroit Symphony Orchestra, then arranger and assistant conductor. He enjoyed the orchestra's regular *Ford Sunday Evening Hour* on the radio and named his second son after the *Hour* and its sponsors, the Ford Motor Company. Eventually he moved back to New York to work for the NBC Symphony Orchestra, then guided by the legendary Arturo Toscanini. He stayed for ten years and his daughter Talia was born in 1946. She recalls the difficult days of her childhood, after Carmine left the NBC Symphony Orchestra: 'My father was very successful when he was younger. Then there was a decade when things were shit. I was growing up in that decade. He was conducting on the road or staying home and being isolated and depressed. I watched him sabotage himself. I watched him be glorious. I travelled on the road with my father when I was nine years old. I know what it means to watch your father's face flush because he's had some applause. I knew that would make him happier than anything I could do. That should have been the decade of my development, the time for having a friend over, and it got lost in concern for my father. I was practically an autistic child – I had a terrific inner world but I was too far inside.'

His father's professional demons also affected Francis Coppola: 'It was a bit like Napoleon's family. At the beginning of memory, as a child of four or five years old, I always ended my prayers with: "Let Daddy get his big break." It was a major theme of my family. One minute we had a little bit of money, the next my father was saying we couldn't afford the mortgage. It was tempestuous. I think most people regard money as a vital element of life: you hold on to it and don't jeopardize it. My attitude toward money is that it is just something to use.'

Nicolas Cage's father August – 'Augie' to the family – was the student idol of the Coppolas, good looking with an engaging, exciting personality. 'Augie was sort of a Renaissance prince,' says his sister Talia. 'In his heyday there was nothing quite like this sort of Tyrone Power guy coming up with these wonderful ideas. He was a true visionary, a pioneer, a philosopher, a cultured man. He told me to read Anaïs Nin when I was twelve. He was always very supportive. Augie is a natural teacher. He would want to see Francis improve and would want to see me improve.'

In the original film version of Mario Puzo's *The Godfather* a Mafia henchman offers his tributes to Marlon Brando's Don Vito Corleone with: 'May their first child be a *masculine* child.' Italia Coppola was always acutely conscious of the importance of her firstborn to the family and she said in 1983: 'August was my first son and he set the example. If it wasn't for August, Francis would be nothing. He was the one who was always helping Francis and doing things for Francis.

'Carmine was very busy, involved with himself and so Francie turned to Augie. This is a hard thing to say but I am going to say it: if Francis had been my first son the family wouldn't be this famous today. Augie was a straight-A student and that made Francie try to get it. If Francis had been the firstborn and had a D on his report card Tallie and Augie wouldn't have given a damn either. Augie is brilliant. I thank God he was the first.'

Francis Coppola acknowledges the truth of this: 'I was funny-looking, not good in school and I didn't know any girls. Augie was great to me and always looked out for me but in addition he did very well in school and received many awards for writing and other things and he was, like, the star in the family. I did most of what I did to imitate him. I even took his short stories and handed them in under my name when I went to my writing class in high school.

'My whole beginning in writing started in copying him, thinking that if I did these things I could be like him. I always wanted to be handsome and smart and a ladies' man like Augie. My father had talent and my brother had talent. I didn't. The issue of talent was an important thing but then I realized that you don't have to have talent, you just have to have a lot of enthusiasm.

August Coppola did not, as his father had hoped, become a medical doctor. He won a Ph.D. in comparative literature and, a pioneer of studies with the blind, taught at California State University at Long Beach where he invented the Tactile Dome. His son Nicolas recalls: 'You crawl in total darkness and feel your way through sponges and netting and you fall into two tons of birdseed or land on a waterbed. But we were going through the exhibit when we were like six and it scared the shit out of me. Looking at it now, it's brilliant. Disneyland wanted him to do one but he wouldn't because he wanted it to be free.'

Later, August became the dean of creative arts at San Francisco

State University. Everything in his life revolved around learning and creativity, which attracted him to the highly strung modern dancer and choreographer Joy Vogelsang. They married in 1960 but the relationship was a turbulent one and ended when Nicolas, the youngest of their three sons, was twelve.

However, while August Coppola excelled as a teacher and academic, his brother Francis's fame grew – so much so that it eclipsed his elder brother. 'Augie's very sensitive to this,' says Talia adding: 'I don't think he wants to deal with it. I'm sure these thoughts occur to him but he *is* a success. He is a remarkable man but there was much pressure on Augie.'

Sibling rivalry occurs often as a theme in Francis Coppola's films but in *The Godfather* movies it is an integral element of the plots. In *The Godfather* it is James Caan's Sonny who leads until, after his death, Al Pacino's Michael takes over. In *Godfather II* it is the late John Cazale's Fredo who betrays the Family and Michael. His explanation for this begins with: 'I'm your older brother and I was passed over.'

Nicolas Kim Coppola was the youngest of August Coppola's sons. His brother Marc, in 1996 a popular New York radio disc jockey on WXRK, known as K-ROCK, arrived in 1961. Christopher, a film director based in Los Angeles, was born a year later, followed by Nicolas in 1964. Although the 'baby' is the most internationally famous of the three, they do not feud. They shared an unconventional upbringing. While other youngsters watched television situation comedies or children's movies, the Coppolas were taken by their father to art house cinemas. Before he was a teenager Nicolas Coppola knew the work of Akira *Seven Samurai* Kurosawa – from whom he took his Japanese phase *and* phrases – and Federico Fellini and other landmark film-makers like Fritz Lang. He was fascinated by silent stars like Lon Chaney, the 'man with a thousand faces', and Max Schreck, the star of F. W. Murnau's 1922 vampire classic *Nosferatu*.

'The other kids were seeing Disney and he was showing us movies like Fellini's *Juliet of the Spirits*.

'At four I used to have this terrible nightmare that I was on the toilet and this giant blonde genie woman in a gold bikini would reach into the bathroom window like King Kong and pluck me off the toilet seat and laugh at me. My father would come into the room while I was screaming and say: "Think of a white horse. The white horse will come and take your bad dreams away." And it did. I would meditate on the white horse. I would visualize it in the dark.

'I had another dream then: a clown scaling a building like Spider-Man. I knew he was coming and I'd look out of the window and he would look up at me and smile at me as he kept on coming. These and other dreams pervaded my childhood. I was scared of many things.'

It was an intense, cultural education. The boys would listen to recordings of their great-grandfather Francesco Pennino and their father educated them about great books and paintings. Cage recalls how one Thanksgiving he and his brothers set the dining table for the family's annual celebratory dinner. They had seen little preparation for the festivities but thought their father was going to spring a surprise. He did. As they settled down at the table he produced paper plates and crayons. Their creative task on that special day was to draw their own dinner. Nicolas gave himself nothing but white meat. *And* extra chestnut stuffing. 'My father sometimes took things a little far. It was kind of fun and interesting but, hey, we were hungry.' He goes on, 'I've always had to deal with things. It started with my mother.'

And his father, who for years had doubts that his youngest son was his own: he thought the actor Robert Mitchum might be the boy's father.

Chapter Three
Worrying Heights

'I think I turned into Heathcliff.'

Nicolas Cage, on moving into his uncle Francis's home in

California's Napa Valley wine country.

The table is laid in old-fashioned Italian style and recipes that haven't been followed in the Old Country for more than fifty years are still in use. The Coppolas enjoy their Genco olive oil, the peppers, tomatoes, pasta, oranges, basil, mozzarella, sun-dried tomatoes in olive oil, and, of course, that staple of Italian cookery, the cannolis. In *The Godfather* when Michael Corleone is being instructed on the finer points of the restaurant execution of a New York police captain the capo Clemenza emphasizes:

'Leave the gun, take the cannolis.'

Francis Coppola bought the Niebaum-Coppola Estate in 1975 for a little more than $2 million, following the box office bonanza of *The Godfather* which other directors had rejected as little more than a 'B' movie. It covers 120 acres of the Napa Valley's most coveted location for Cabernet Sauvignon. 'It was a lucky accident,' says Coppola. 'I felt an obligation to the estate's founder Gustave Niebaum who began making fine wine here in the 1880s. I wanted to carry on the tradition. But most importantly I bought the property as a place in the country for my family.'

And that family included his brother Augie's youngest boy.

Nicolas Cage was six when he first became aware of the troubles that would lead him later to the Napa Valley. The family lived in a suburban, middle-class area of Long Beach and then around Los Angeles, but August Coppola was more interested in his teaching than in wealth.

His wife worried him: she was increasingly troubled by severe periods of depression and her son still finds it difficult to talk about his mother's mental health problems: 'She would go away for years at a time. When she got too erratic she went to the . . . she went away. Then my childhood consisted of going to see her. And that hallway was a long hallway, let me tell you, going in there with the crazy people who would be touching and – it was very arresting. She was plagued with mental illness for most of my childhood. She was institutionalized for years and went through shock treatments.

'She went through these episodes of poetry – I don't know what else to call it. She would say the most amazing things, beautiful but scary. I'm sure they had an impact on me. If I look at home movies of when I was two years old I see that she was a very caring mother – the way she touched me. I remember one birthday when I was scared by all the candles. I'd try to run away and she would turn me back. It was very beautiful. But the hardest part was going to visit her in the institutions. I was quite young. As I said there was a long hallway we had to walk down to see Mom, past people grabbing at us. At the end of it she was always there, sitting, waiting. Sometimes she would go into Rip Van Winkle mode and forget everything that had happened, that her father had died or I had become an actor. She's fine now but much time was lost.

'The strangest thing about it is that even when things got really bizarre I was able to detach and look at it with a scientific curiosity. I'm sure it had some impact on me, though. And maybe her illness was behind the nightmares I had – but I always felt protected. She never wanted to hurt anybody. The hardest part was seeing someone I love suffer.

'It hurt my father too. He stayed married for sixteen years, trying to make it work, and that's a heck of a situation. His blood pressure went up and he did most of the raising of us. It was really hard on him. I wouldn't change it for anything in one way: I think it made my life rich and gave me a depth of emotion. It's like a blessing in disguise. I gained something from it. It gave me an insight and a sensitivity that I don't think I would have had.

'When I was six years old I wanted to figure out ways of getting inside a television set. I would be sitting on my living room floor and there was our 1965 television set. It was this beautiful little Zenith TV that was wood and had an oval screen. I would sit there just wishing I could get inside that TV. That was when I first realized I wanted to be an actor. I was so mystified by the tiny people. Dinosaurs were inside the TV, and Jerry Lewis. I do so remember sitting there on the red carpet, a round throw rug, and wanting to murder Mr Gree Jeans who was the most boring thing about the *Captain Kangaroo* show.'

In 1996 he found that television set. He asked his maternal grandmother Louise Vogelsang (known as Divi to the family) if it was still around and, somehow, it turned up. Cage likes the past. Back then he also found escape in his brother Christopher's Super-8 movies. Christopher says: 'Nic was my leading man when he was about eight. He really put himself into these movies. He loved it, always loved it. He was a natural performer. There was nothing he didn't want to to try and do.'

When Nicolas was alone he would sit on a swing in the garden: 'I would watch the clouds and imagine I could see Pinocchio peering down from above. When I was four my father took me to the town in Italy where the author of Pinocchio was born. All they did there was sell Pinocchios. I still have one. The story parallels my life a bit. The whole bit about "an actor's life for me". Being a puppet who loses his strings. I must have been in my own world. I was probably trying to get away from whatever crisis was happening at home so I had this tremendous imagination and an ability to reinvent myself. I just started playing real hard.

'I wanted to be in disguise. I thought the coolest thing you could do was dress yourself up as somebody else. I loved Hallowe'en and costumes. As a child in Long Beach I spent a lot of time pretending I was other people. I was into the whole concept of trying to disguise myself. In the 1970s on TV *Toma* [which starred Tony Musante] was this disguise-artist detective and I thought that was *very* cool. I used to disguise myself going to school to keep from getting beaten up on the bus.

'And my father helped that. He was always doing things to encourage our imaginations. I remember my father as being this Sean-Connery-as-James-Bond type. When he took me to see *Dr No* at the drive-in, I imagined myself as James Bond's son. I learned some of what being a man was about by watching James Bond. I now realize that it's other things – more important other things. But I loved that image. My father had this very professorial air about him but he always approached things with a great deal of creativity.

'I was expelled from regular elementary school for being a prankster: the kids all brought lunch to class and I said bring egg salad sandwiches. I went to Farmer's Market [a Chinatown supermarket] and bought five cans of fried grasshoppers and crushed 'em up, put 'em in the egg salad and watched everybody eat the grasshoppers. They'd go: "Oh, there's an antenna in there!" Well, I got caught and expelled and I went to a very rough school, which was where I used to get beat up at the back of the bus because there were these three big guys who commandeered the back seat. I was in fourth grade, about nine or ten. They were twelve and thirteen. One day I'd had enough. I got some black Ray-Ban sunglasses and I stuck some chewing gum in my mouth and I got my older brother's cowboy boots on and some tight jeans and had this swagger when I got on the bus. I said I was Roy Richards and "I'm Nicky Coppola's cousin and if you screw with him again I'm going to kick your ass. If you keep bothering him I'm gonna kick your ass." It worked. They *bought* it. They never beat up on me again. It was really my first experience with acting, with changing myself. I learned I could act – and there was power in being able to act.'

He has told the story before but he insists it is not some public-relations fantasy: 'It absolutely happened. I did it another time, too. There was another neighbourhood bully who was always beating me and my older brothers up. One day I became the Incredible Hulk. I took my shirt off and screamed as loud as I could and chased him. I was just a skinny little runt but he ran off. There's power in acting.'

And, of course, escape.

He found another escape in being the playground and class clown. It did not sit well with his teachers and he moved from one Long Beach elementary school to another. Academically he was fine: his personality was the problem.

His father tried to compensate for his mother's illness: 'One time

I was upset about breaking my little Pinocchio toy. So my father planted Pinocchio's head in the garden and told me to water it. A couple of days later a great big plant-like thing had grown in its place. I ran out and it was a giant wooden Pinocchio that my father had placed there. After that I started planting all my hot-wheel cars with the hope one of them would blossom into a real car but it never quite worked the same.

'Seeing *Frankenstein* gave me ideas. Once I tried to save a dying Christmas tree by trying to sew and tape its trunk to the roots of a live tree. I felt so bad for that Christmas tree that I killed another tree trying to bring it back to life.'

However, other things didn't mend: he was twelve when his parents divorced. 'It was a sad day but it was a good day. I remember my mother wanting to have custody and I knew she loved us. It wasn't traumatic. I was relieved. It was uncomfortable, though. I had to sit down and talk with the judge. I went in and smiled the whole way through the meeting. It was sad about the custody because my mother obviously wasn't able to raise us yet she still tried to be strong and have dignity, and she wanted custody.

'You know, you see shows like *The Brady Bunch* and they paint these pictures of a family without problems. That's not fair. It makes everybody feel like they are abnormal. My mother's fine now and very jolly with a terrific sense of humour. She's always had a wonderful imagination. She's been a huge inspiration in my work because she was just naturally kind of surreal.'

He created such a world for himself: 'Because of my father's creative encouragement, as well as growing up in a broken home, I invented a fantasy world. I remember when I was nine or ten and crazy about comic books I came up with a comic book *alter ego*. I called myself "The Spirit" and I would put on this white T-shirt with a black S on it, a white fedora hat and a white cape and I'd strap a boomerang to my chest. Every night at around two in the morning I would climb out of my window and wander the alley behind my house looking for evil-doers with my boomerang.

'Then, I thought I was the daredevil Evel Knievel. I saw George Hamilton play him in the movie and I remember thinking how cool he was, the way he would rev his bike, adjust the chain, wipe the grease off his boot – all in slow motion – then do the ultimate jump over twenty vans. That changed my life. From then on I started jumping over beer kegs with my bicycle. But that wasn't enough. So one day I made a big hoop of cardboard and doused it in kerosene and announced to the whole neighbourhood that I was going to jump through this hoop of fire. Word quickly got out and all these kids started paying money to watch me do it. But when the big day came my dad found out about it and shut the whole thing down.

'But I was really going to do it. There were never a question in my mind. Growing up I spent a lot of time in my mind. To me Pete Townsend of The Who was a medieval knight. I saw Bruce Lee movies and wanted to be him very badly so I started working out when I was twelve. I used to do all these sit-ups in the morning and then go to school. I studied Kung Fu as well. I was so angry.'

In 1976, August Coppola moved his family to the outskirts of Beverly Hills. He found a house on La Cienega and Hamilton Drive so that he could take advantage of the city's superior school system.

The first two *Godfather* films, the award-winning *The Conversation* and the landmark happy-days movie *American Graffiti* had made Nicolas' uncle Francis fabulously well known and rich. But Nicolas was the elder brother's youngest son: 'We didn't have a lot of money. I didn't have money. It was frustrating to me that people would say: "You're Francis Ford Coppola's nephew, why don't you drive a sports car?"'

'I didn't like high school. I was a nerd and I didn't fit in. I went to Beverly Hills High [the school in which *Beverly Hills 90210* is set] and I hate saying that because it suggests I came from a rich family. The truth is my father was supporting three children on a teacher's salary. Going to a school like Beverly Hills High where all the kids have money, and they're driving to school in Porsches and Ferraris and I'm taking the RTD bus, and I can't ask a girl out because I'd have to ask her to take the bus with me – well, it was frustrating to say the least. I grew up in the car culture.

'I got my first Triumph Spitfire when I was sixteen and my father wouldn't let me drive it. I would sit in the car and pretend to drive it.

In the meantime he would drive it. I bought it with my own money but I had to watch him drive it with the top down. I would have to pretend that I was driving.

'Finally, I got it registered and the car didn't want to work. It was always breaking down and I was always dragging it into the shop. On Prom Night I had a date. My grandmother had given me and my brothers saving bonds. One brother cashed his bonds and got a stereo system. My other brother bought a used car. I cashed my bonds and rented a tuxedo and a limousine so I could take this beautiful girl to the Prom. We're at the Prom and I kissed her. When she responded I was so nervous I started throwing up. The limousine driver wouldn't let me back into the limousine because there was vomit on my shoes. So I walked home. That was my Prom.

'A lot of problems I have with Hollywood are the same ones I had with high school: it's basically a popularity contest. It's all about who's going out with whom, who's the prettiest, who the funniest, who's the best.' At the time, the celebrated Francis Ford Coppolas were the tops.

When Nicolas's elder brothers left home, his father planned a lecture tour of America: Nicolas would live with his uncle's family in Napa. It proved a formative experience that confirmed Nicolas Cage as a loner, an outsider: 'I felt like: "Why is it that they have all this stuff and my brothers and I don't? I want to get some of that." I was in this wonderful house with wonderfully generous people but it wasn't *my* stuff, it wasn't *my* house. I didn't know why I was there. I was frustrated beyond belief, man . . .'

His father had given him books like *Brave New World* and *Siddhartha* and, Cage remembers, 'He would say: "I want you to pretend you are inside the book and I want you to use the characters and the situations and write a chapter that doesn't exist."'

In a way, that is what he did while he lived at the Coppola estate: 'I turned into Heathcliff. I felt a *Wuthering Heights* sort of drive. I've had a strange relationship with money because I've seen it from an early age and seen its powerful effects. It was like a golden key was given to me because I said: "You know what? I am going to get back. I am going to get even somehow. I said I was going to buy a *big* house in San Francisco where they [Francis Coppola's family] had one and I did. I vowed then that I would go to Los Angeles, learn to act, and then one day buy my own Victorian mansion in San Francisco. Like Heathcliff, I was the outsider. No, I *felt* the outsider, the one who was different. It was just sort of unfortunate that it was revenge that fuelled much of my ambition.'

'Nicolas was always fascinating,' says Francis Coppola. 'Even when he was little he was at the heart of fascinating routines: the "Oh, Computer" routine and "The Cheese Man". He would repeat the same phrase again and again: each time it became more hilarious. He went on to prove so much. He *is* a Coppola. Nicolas has his own identity and wanted to accentuate that. My thought then and now is that he is a Coppola and we are proud of him and wish his name was still Coppola.'

But, unlike Heathcliff in *Wuthering Heights*, the bitterness young Nicolas felt had a positive result. In Los Angeles he attended the drama department of Beverly Hills High. He had told his father he wanted to become a writer: 'That made him very happy and he encouraged me to write all the time.

'I was into acting, though, and one day I came home late because I had been auditioning for a new play. As a result the dishes didn't get washed. My father was furious: "You're never going to become an *actor*, Nicolas! Why don't you just forget it!" It was the one time I stood up to my father. I just lost it. I blew up at him. I started yelling and screaming and all this rage came pouring out. It was a real day of anger. I said: "You're wrong. I *am* going to be an actor." Later he said he did it to make me want to prove him wrong but I don't believe him. There was always this strange dynamic with my father. He's given me so much in terms of my ability to look at the world in a special way because he's a great thinker but at the same time there's this thing.

'My father, like anybody, has more than one side. He was very into the creative stuff but he could also be verbally abusive. To be perfectly honest I needed to believe he believed in me. If he thought I was special I would have the courage to get on with what I wanted to do with my life. But there was the *thing*. I don't know how to explain it but it had something to do with my mother telling him I wasn't his kid. She had a signed photograph of Robert Mitchum and always made hints. That beautiful old photograph of Robert Mitchum says: "To Joy, Love and Kisses, Bob". Obviously, nothing happened. She was just a young lady in a dance group and Mitchum was around and she got an autographed picture. But my dad used to always bring him up. So, consequently I became a Mitchum fan. I'd watch his movies and say: "What is it about this guy that my father finds so interesting?" You know: "Should I study him?"

'The Mitchum business started when they were fighting and she wanted to get a rise out of him. She said to him: "Nicky's not your child." She admitted to me that she told him that in the heat of anger. I'm sure she doesn't feel good about it but you know how people say things in the heat of anger. But I said: "I've lived with that anger from my father for thirty years." The fact is that if you look at a picture of my dad and you look at me it's obvious that I'm his son. But there has always been an edge from my father toward me and that must be the reason.'

All the anger and frustration produced powerful energy as well as ambition in the young Cage. His father and brothers say they noticed a 'steeliness' in him. 'There was a certain resolve,' says his brother Marc. 'With Nic you knew that his determination would get him what he wanted.'

He wanted revenge. And for that he needed fame. He wanted to make a name for himself in Los Angeles on his own merit but was never above picking his uncle's brains. 'Sometimes I'd ask him questions about people he had worked with. Once, I asked him about auditions because I was having trouble with readings. He reminded me that the reading is not the finished product and that has always calmed me down. He told me how Brando used to like to work with the artificial elements around him on films like *Mutiny on the Bounty*, where he requested a block of ice to sit on for his death scene so he would be shivering the shivers of death. These are probably all secrets. I shouldn't be exposing them . . .'

But it was Al Pacino in a scene from *The Godfather* who most affected him. When the film was released in America, Uncle Francis sent his nephew a bundle of promotional T-shirts but his father, sibling rivalry glaringly obvious, forbade young Nicolas to wear them or to see the film. However, Cage sneaked off to a screening of the movie and he recalls: 'There was that scene where Al Pacino kisses the beautiful Sicilian woman and she takes her bra off. I remember I was feeling new things. It really turned me on.'

But sexual fantasy had arrived earlier – in the form of Barbara Eden as the genie opposite Larry Hagman's astronaut in the television series *I Dream of Jeannie*. 'That caused me a great deal of difficulty in my life. The Barbara Eden fantasy. Because when you follow the *Jeannie* course you're in trouble. There are women who know how to *play* the *Jeannie* role and use it as a net: the perfect woman who will do anything for you and will make magical things happen. Then they catch you and you're the one stuck inside the bottle.'

But they were never going to be able to cork up Nicolas Cage.

Chapter Four
Rumbled

'We come from a long line of robbers and highwaymen.'

Nicolas Cage, on family roots.

Nicolas Cage has become the odd-man-out of American film, the screwball, the neo-expressionist attraction who has won millions of passionate fans. That he has done so, against the conservative number-crunching of Hollywood, is a tribute to his cavalier history and what one US critic summed up as the 'riotous energy of his outward charm'.

Having sworn to himself that an acting career would be his revenge for his poverty-stricken childhood and his salvation, he began to work at it and he is a dedicated worker. He is his father's son: learning is everything. He was taken by the father-son relationship in director Elia Kazan's 1955 movie version of John Steinbeck's *East of Eden*. The film established the young James Dean – desperate for and *needing* the love and approval of father Raymond Massey – as a rebel. Cage identified with everything about the movie.

He enrolled for a summer course in character development at San Francisco's American Conservatory Theatre and appeared in a production of *Golden Boy*, the boxing story that in 1939 had made a film star of William Holden. Nicolas was fifteen and everything seemed possible: 'He believed he could do it, he believed in himself and that's the great gift he has,' says his brother Marc. 'Nicolas was never going to fail – he would never allow himself to do that,' said Francis Coppola.

But, initially, failure was his spur.

He had been in the theatre group at Beverly Hills High but he didn't win a leading role in a student production of *West Side Story*.

He was in his senior year and dropped out after he had passed the General Educational Development test. 'He wasn't the best student but he was well liked by the other kids and the staff,' said Welsh-born Julia Maggs, the then headmaster's secretary. She added: 'There were plenty of students with lots of money and connections but he kept his background quiet. When you look back on the situation now it really seems he wanted to make it on his own. He certainly had the confidence and it has paid off. He's a credit to the school. He's worked hard for what he has achieved and that's what education is about: setting your goals and going for them.'

Personal manager Chris Viores had spotted Cage in a school production of *Oklahoma* and encouraged him to audition for television series. The *Baywatch* of the day was the rather sad *The Best of Times*, and Cage won the role of a body-building surfer. It was not typecasting. 'I was seventeen when I got the part. It was a very bad television show but me just getting the part surprised everyone because I'd kept it to myself what I was up to. It wasn't very good but I still feel proud about it because it was something that happened of its own accord. And it did the job. The family gradually warmed up to me being an actor.'

He instantly joined the generic 'Brat Pack' when he landed a role in director Amy Heckerling's now classic teenage comedy *Fast Times at Ridgemont High*. In it Sean Penn played *the* doped-out Californian surfer in a classroom of goofballs. It was 1982 and seventeen-year-old Cage lost out to Judge Reinhold – who went on to bigger roles and money with Eddie Murphy in the *Beverly Hills Cop* movies – for the part of Brad. Instead, he was hired and screen-listed as 'Brad's buddy', numbered twenty-first in the cast list. It certainly wasn't a huge part and what there was was mostly lost in the cutting room. But he learned about acting – and the envy and cruelty of other people. 'I would watch Sean Penn and try to get ideas. He was so good and so confident. I was pretty much the nerd to everybody. My fellow actors didn't accept me. People would ask for me to be removed from their eyeline when they were on camera. I was the brunt of jokes because my name was still Coppola. They said I was there because of Francis Coppola. These actors know who they are. I know who they are. I felt the burden of being his nephew. On the set of *Fast Times at Ridgemont High* the actors would congregate outside my trailer and recite a version of Robert Duvall's line from *Apocalypse Now*. In my uncle's film he said: "I love the smell of napalm in the morning." They changed it to: "I love the smell of Nicolas in the morning." It was psychologically hard. No matter how good you are you feel you're not good enough. So I really had something to prove to others. See, I knew something nobody else could possibly know. I knew I wanted to act long before I knew anything else. But I felt I had to work twice as hard as the next guy to prove myself.

'Being a Coppola was a mixed blessing. Francis is a powerful man who enjoys his position.' Most appropriately Luciano Pavarotti played him in a movie: everything about Francis Ford Coppola's life has been on a grand scale. Even his bankruptcy was of operatic style and proportions.

The film-maker who once flew from California to London 'for lunch' is a bear of a man with a pasta stomach and a salt and pepper beard. In 1980, he created his own film studio, Zoetrope, and from it in 1982 emerged *One from the Heart*, starring Coppola favourite Frederic Forrest, Nastassja Kinski and Teri Garr. Zoetrope, Coppola admitted, could not survive a commercial disaster and *One from the Heart* belly-flopped at the box office, putting Coppola at the centre of a financial labyrinth that tower blocks of lawyers found themselves attempting to sort out.

Coppola's answer to money problems is to work. He had the film rights to two of novelist S.H. Hinton's books aimed at young adults, *The Outsiders* and *Rumble Fish*.

While he was filming *The Outsiders* in Tulsa, Oklahoma, he decided to make *Rumble Fish* at the same time. 'While we were shooting *The Outsiders* I was writing the screenplay for *Rumble Fish*. No one took me seriously but I said I was going to make it.' He dedicated the film: 'To my older brother August Coppola, my first and best teacher'.

Rumble Fish is about a tragic triangle formed by a father, played by Dennis Hopper, and his two sons, the cool motorcycle-riding Mickey Rourke and the wannabe-cool Matt Dillon. 'You ain't gonna be like him, your brother is a prince,' another character tells Dillon, who is jealous that his mother preferred his older brother.

Coppola says the film is 'very personal' and adds: 'It does come out of a certain period of my life when I was about seven, eight and nine. I have a brother five years older who was my idol, who was very, very good to me. Just took me everywhere and taught me everything. He was the leader of the gang and he was tremendously handsome – still is.'

While Francis was coping with the moneymen his nephew was looking for work: 'Directors and casting agents didn't want to know me because of my surname. They used to say "Well, this guy's connected – we don't want to give him a shot."'

His uncle did. But it wasn't straight nepotism. Cage had auditioned for *The Outsiders* and been kept waiting for seven hours before being turned down. But in *Rumble Fish* Francis believed he had a role for his nephew. Cage recalls: 'It was interesting. Francis asked me to rehearse some actors. So, I wasn't auditioning, I was there *reading* Mickey Rourke and Matt Dillon. The next day I found out I had a job and it really blew my mind. That was really high pressure. Here I was, the nephew of the director, without any more under my belt to speak of and that made the other actors nervous. I felt this pressure to pull it off. When I look back I think it is one of the better things I've ever done.'

Cage was cast as Smokey, the friend of troubled Matt Dillon, and he discovered that working with family was a rough ride. His uncle made him repeat a scene where he glances at his watch, forty-one times. Cage did not openly resent it for he had joined a group of young talent, including Sean Penn's brother Christopher, Vincent Spano, Laurence Fishburne and Diane Lane. The performances Coppola coaxed from them were applauded – and overshadowed the impact of the film, which remains an underrated gem: an *American* art film. It remains dear to Francis Coppola and he enthusiastically pointed to a detail that meant much to him but was certainly overlooked by everyone except perhaps his most immediate family: 'That relationship with my brother was a powerful part of my childhood. I had a dream once as a kid that scared me to death. I was in this street and there was this enormous manhole, and these tough kids were getting my brother and putting him in there and were going to cover him with this manhole cover. And I ran to the house to get a phone call to the cops. I never forgot that dream. And these streets in *Rumble Fish* were the same streets as in the dream. That jacket in the movie that Nicolas wears, that wild goose jacket? That was *his* jacket, my brother's. It was a copy of his real one.

'He had such a magical allure that when I read *Rumble Fish* I recalled that. I would say that my love for my brother formed the majority of aspects of what I am.'

In a way, Nicolas Cage says, he still believes in Santa Claus. But back then he mostly believed in himself. He had to. No one else did and certainly not Matt Dillon. Then Cage called his co-star an airhead but says now: 'I don't think of Matt Dillon as an airhead. He's a darn good actor. The funny thing about growing up in the movies is when you start acting at seventeen you say things sometimes like a seventeen-year-old and those things come back to haunt you when you're older. People have to be allowed to grow.'

Which is exactly what he felt back then – that he wanted to *grow*. He also wanted to divorce himself from his uncle, which he did by changing his name. But blood ties – especially the Italian variety – cannot be wiped out by deed poll.

As always when he was most confused Cage went to see his maternal grandmother. He sat at Divi's kitchen table and they worked out a new name for him. They both liked *Vogel.* He fancied Nick *Masccalzone* – 'bad boy' in Italian. Then he was going to be Nic Blue after his favourite colour, and Nic Faust, but whose soul was he selling?

Depending on his mood, Cage came from either his favourite comic-book hero, the African-American adventurer Luke Cage Power, or the composer John Cage, whom his father much admired.

Although he and Divi liked Nicolas Cage the rest of the family did not: his uncle sent him a telegram of congratulations and signed it *Francis Cage.* But it had to be done: 'When I first started going to auditions and was using my real name it was obvious that people were thinking about twenty years of someone else's history. I just wanted to go into an office and just do what I had to do. As Nic Cage, the first audition I did was the best audition I'd ever had. That told me I'd done the right thing.'

The movie was *Valley Girl* – yet another take on *Romeo and Juliet* – and the director was the distinguished Martha Coolidge. Cage went up for the James-Dean-type role of the north Hollywood punk Randy and got it. It was 1983.

Deborah Foreman starred as Julie, a strawberry of a middle-class girl from the San Fernando Valley suburb of Los Angeles who has split up with her athlete boyfriend, Tommy, played by Michael Bowen. It is then that she meets Cage's Randy – the actor was praised for his 'dopey sexuality' – the offbeat, moony newcomer from the other, and wrong, side of the tracks. Julie has to choose between the 'awesome' jock and new-wave Randy. Her friends don't see the choice between Mr Atlas and Mr Creepy but in Coolidge's satire there's no contest.

Cage had hired agent Ilene Feldman to do his talking – Robert De Niro, Al Pacino, Sean Penn, Harrison Ford, didn't do publicity, give interviews to magazines – and she did: 'To Nic acting is just a job. He wants to do his best. If people want to write about his work on screen he thinks that's fine. He just doesn't want to exploit himself.'

She goes on: 'After *Valley Girl* there was a tremendous amount of interest in him. He seemed to be being brought up for every project that was around. His money went up but he didn't want to acknowledge his new popularity. He was still insecure about readings. He didn't want to capitalize on the Coppola name and he thought it was extremely unfair that people mentioned it. But, of course, they did. Why wouldn't they? He was a little naïve then. But he was young. He signed on with me under the name Nicolas Cage. When Martha Coolidge auditioned him she had no idea who he was – only that he had a small part in *Rumble Fish*.' Later, Coolidge admitted that if she had known his 'true' identity it would have coloured her decision.

When he was enthusiastically preparing for his role Cage decided on some Method preparation. He is well endowed with body hair and shaved that on his chest into a traingle shape to get what he calls 'that Superman look'.

In the early years Cage was genuinely reticent about publicity but nevertheless retained his flair for doing something different. He had it 'leaked', through Ilene Feldman, to the *Los Angeles Times*, which amounts to Hollywood's house newspaper, that he owned a two-and-a-half-foot-long monitor lizard, named Smokey after his *Rumble Fish* character. He didn't let out that when he changed his name, he had also had a lizard, eight inches long with a top hat, cane and flute, tattooed on his back. 'It was a stupid rationalization – like, I will never have to take my shirt off in a movie again – at a time when I felt I could have fallen into the trap of being the "beefcake hunk". More important I was claiming my own body and my own right as a man over myself in a circumstance where my father would see it. When he did, he went, "Oh, my God," and his face turned white. It was a good moment. Like a metamorphosis.'

Indeed, that was what was happening. *Valley Girl* led him to *Racing with the Moon* – this time he was Sean Penn's buddy – and then came *The Cotton Club* with his uncle. He went for that even though Ilene Feldman warned him that it would again provoke claims that he had been given the role because of his family connections.

There was a lot of talent around but Nicolas Cage seemed to be the only one who either wanted or was willing to be the leading character actor as opposed to the leading man. He was running with and against brothers Charlie Sheen and Emilio Estevez (sons of Martin Sheen), Kiefer Sutherland (son of Donald), Robert Downey Junior, soul mate Crispin Glover (they had been schoolmates at Beverly Hills High), Matthew Modine, Tom Cruise, Timothy Hutton, Judd Nelson, Rob Lowe, Nastassja Kinski, Demi Moore, Molly Ringwald, Ally Sheedy, Matthew Broderick, Andrew McCarthy, Ralph Macchio, C. Thomas Howell, Kevin Bacon, Rebecca de Mornay and Laura Dern. They were not a crowd to have illusions: most had grown up with the movie industry. They were hip and their disdain sometimes bordered on nihilism. Of course, the Kurt Cobain attitude only made them more popular with their own generation and with movie-goers who had tired of the teenage films being produced throughout the 1980s. The group broadcast attitude – but there was integrity, too, about the Brat Pack. Sean Penn – whom Cage calls 'an inspirational figure' and of whom he says that he was as influential on his professional life as

Jack Nicholson – and Cage broke away from the Pack. They refused to play the Hollywood game and it paid off.

Chapter Five
Penn Friend

'I've never been into perfection. I like the faults that people have.'

Nicolas Cage, 1996.

t was 2 May 1983, and Nicolas Cage thought he had stumbled into Paradise. He was on location with *Racing with the Moon* on California's rugged coast in and around Mendocino. California may be America's most populated state but here it is isolated with tiny groups of clapboard cottages and small shops spread across the rise leading from the cliffs. It is a four-hour drive from San Francisco, through the forests of giant redwoods to Mendocino, and you can get there by light aircraft but frequent fog along the coastline makes that haphazard.

Cage was in his element. The location, with its unobstructed view of rolling Pacific surf and fields blanketed with wild flowers, had been used before and most memorably for the opening sequence of *East of Eden* when James Dean arrives at the small coastal town looking for his mother.

Cage's co-star was Sean Penn, and Sherry Lansing, the co-producer and former actress, who became the first woman to head a major Hollywood studio – 20th Century Fox – had personally wanted him for role of Penn's Second World War sidekick. She recalled: 'I had seen *Valley Girl* and thought Nic had just the right look and feel for our Nicky in the movie. Sean's a strong character and we needed someone who wouldn't be overshadowed by him. He had to be a buffer but also have his own energy. We – and certainly the critics – never complained about the casting.'

In the film it is 1942 and the Second World War – for the Americans – had entered its second year. Penn, as Hopper, and Cage, as his friend Nicky, have enlisted in the US Marines. They are preparing to leave their home town of Point Muir. Hopper has a solid family but Nicky's mother has died and his father is mentally and physically abusing him. Hopper is in love with Elizabeth McGovern (Penn and McGovern enjoyed an off-screen romance, which resulted in a short-term engagement) while Nicky's girlfriend, played by Julie Phillips, is pregnant and they are seeking an abortion.

This slightly soap-opera story of the coming of age of two friends was a perfect vehicle for Penn and Cage. The movie included a sequence of the young men playing their childhood game of grabbing the rail on freight trains to hitch rides. Off-screen Cage and Penn played their own game: 'There's one shot where Sean and I are standing in front of an oncoming train and have to jump out of the way at the right time. We got into this stand-off – who was going to jump first? It was good-natured but definitely a macho, boys'-day-out attitude between us.

'I have the utmost respect for Sean. By working with him and watching how he handled his life and career I think that gave me a handle on how to deal with the things. With the pressure. And he had a lot of that – especially when he fell in love with Madonna.'

Penn is a 'a poet and not a simple person' according to actress Anjelica Huston, and she sees 'a certain male mythology about him, a mixture of tenderness and pugnaciousness that's prevalent in the Irish and causes them to stay up late drinking whisky, writing poetry, getting into fights and falling in love with cool, blonde women who'll drive them crazy' – maybe that's something else the two actors have in common.

Over the years Cage and Penn have kept in contact; often they found themselves interested in the same projects. But the main link between them in the early years was their ongoing estrangement from conventional Hollywood. The two stars have learned from each other how to play the fame game. They have gone from brats to grown-ups. Penn was a Midas of a mentor. Cage agrees that he and Penn have mellowed but argues: 'We know that there's a fifty per cent chance that death is probably going to be a trip, a roller-coaster. Personally my motto has always been: "Stick around, it might turn out to be funny." We're all going to die anyway.'

'They're not that different,' said producer Michael Bergman. 'They're both very intense. It's Method to them and Sean may be the master.'

When Penn was preparing for *Bad Boys* he went out on a Chicago police raid. Director Richard Rosenthal recalled: 'We were filming when some police arrived and thought we were criminals and told us to raise our hands. Sean thought this was an opportunity: what it's like for a gang member to take on a cop? So he turned to the cop the size of an apartment building and said: "*Fuck you.*"

'The cop picked Sean up and threw him into a wall. His nose was almost broken but later he told me it was at that moment that he finally made the transition to becoming the character.'

Cage takes up the Method idea: 'I started acting at an early age and didn't have proper training, I was doing what I thought my heroes would do – Marlon Brando, Montgomery Clift, Robert De Niro, Cary Grant. I wanted to be living the part. The way that Clift stayed up all night to do a scene in which he was tired or De Niro gained forty or fifty pounds to play Jake LaMotta in *Raging Bull*, Brando on the block of ice in his death scene in *Mutiny on the Bounty*. That kind of stuff. That reckless, adventurous style was fun and fascinating.'

Cage enjoyed the strong friendship he began to build with Penn in Mendocino and was sorrry to reach the end of the six weeks' location filming. But there was more work to do on the sound stages at Paramount Studios on the film, and he was about to start work on *The Cotton Club*. In 1971 Francis Coppola had been offered the director's job on *The Godfather* by the producer Robert Evans and the book's author Mario Puzo. Now, in 1983 the two men were making a similar offer, one that Coppola found he 'couldn't refuse'. He would receive $2.5 million for directing and writing a new script for *The Cotton Club*.

The prospect of bringing off the tale of music and mobsters in 1920s Harlem was daunting. Coppola reshaped the screenplay around a story of two sets of brothers, his familiar theme. Gregory and Maurice Hines comprised one pair while Richard Gere and Nicolas Cage were the other. And Cage was not the only family member around to give Coppola a feeling of security: Francis's sons,

Gian-Carlo and Roman, were taken on as production assistants. But it was Cage who had to make his presence felt on screen in a film that dealt with guns, murder and drugs. He explains his role: 'He's so maniacally up he's almost in outer space. At times I felt I had to hold on to my own head to keep it from hitting the ceiling. The guy's an empty balloon with a hell of a lot of unsuspected energy. As mad as they come. Mad Dog – Mad Dog Dwyer – is what they call him in the movie.'

They said that about Cage and several others off-screen, too, for on *The Cotton Club* madness was in the air.

Chapter Six
Nose Candy

'I went for help to people I had made millions of dollars for and they turned me down.' Robert Evans, on *The Cotton Club* troubles.

A thick, foul fog belched from the smoke machines over the nightclub crowd and the movie extras held white silk handkerchiefs to their faces. All around, men in slick black ties and slicker hair, carnations at attention in their lapels, lounged, as instructed, like lizards. Women squeezed into sequinned affairs squealed and preened over the waterfalls of champagne splashing into their glasses. On a stage ringed with pink and turquoise lights, flappers with tight brown stomachs went through routines as endless as the ranks of legs in satin shoes. '*OK, ready, roll!*' The all-black chorus launched into another leggy number for Francis Coppola's cameras.

Nicolas Cage watched the action from the wings of the reconstructed Astoria Studio in Queens, New York, where a replica of the Cotton Club, the elegant and celebrated nightspot of Harlem's Jazz Age, had been created for a film that was seen as a $45 million return to the classic gangster movies of Hollywood, to the days of the squires of the genre, like James Cagney, George Raft, Edward G. Robinson and Pat O'Brien.

The first complication that arose was the confusion as to whether *The Cotton Club* was a gangster picture or a musical. It became an uneasy mix of both.

In the Prohibition era Edwina Mountbatten called the club the 'aristocrat of Harlem' and doted on the dark-skinned performers of both sexes. The performers were black, the clientele white. Officially the high-society crowds who got their thrills slumming in Harlem, guzzling illegal booze and fraternising with hoodlums, didn't mix with the help. Guests included Jimmy Durante, Irving Berlin, Milton Berle, Samuel Goldwyn, Fanny 'Funny Girl' Brice, Joan Crawford, Gloria Swanson, Joseph Kennedy, Babe Ruth, James Cagney and Tallulah Bankhead. The club was founded by Yorkshire-born Owney Madden while he was still in his cell in Sing Sing. Duke Ellington and the Washingtonians played there. A bouncer once grabbed the head of Lena Horne's stepfather and shoved it down a toilet.

That incident, Ellington, played by Zane Mark, and Owney Madden, Bob Hoskins, wove in and out of the movie story Robert Evans always called '*The Godfather* with music: music, sex and gangsters'.

The material was rich; Coppola saw that immediately he was approached by Robert Evans to work on the script: 'Bob Evans inspires people to want to take care of him – maybe because he's like a reckless prince or something,' recalls Coppola of his early involvement in *The Cotton Club*.

'At any rate he's gotten in trouble a couple of times and I'd always felt compelled to help him. He called me in desperation with some hokey metaphor about his baby being sick and needing a doctor. Bottom line, I said I'd be happy to help him for a week or so, no charge, to see if I could give him an opinion. I was just thinking that maybe the script was a little screwed. And I looked at it and I saw there was nothing I could do in a week. There was nothing there: it was a shallow gangster story without an attempt to do anything.

'But in reading some of the research I started to become ... there's a lot going on in that period and it's very stimulating. It has music and it has theatre, great theatre, and it has beautiful dancers. So I took a shot at the script, I reworked it. Evans kept offering for me to direct it and I didn't want to because I was terrified of being in a situation where I have people second-guessing me. Because my ideas don't sound good when I first say them and they always sound really good later if I'm allowed to do them. But if I have to fight for everything like I had to fight for Al Pacino and Marlon Brando on *The Godfather* I can't put up with that. I made it clear that I would need to control it at every possible level. If I had control there was no reason why I couldn't make a beautiful film out of it ...'

Jerry Wexler, the music director who was fired by Coppola, now calls the project 'a mammoth train wreck waiting to happen'. Evans and Coppola feuded. The budget and paranoia grew. Two investors, Las Vegas casino owners Ed and Fred Doumani, got nervous: the film was costing $250,000 a day to make. Coppola wanted the film to be anything but the conventional gangster story that Evans had envisaged and fired five of Evans's production staff.

There were thirty-nine scripts for *The Cotton Club* – all produced on different shades of paper. It was known as 'the rainbow script'. The film was nearly cancelled because money kept running out. Coppola and Richard Gere both walked off the set at different times. Evans took the moneymen to court to regain some control.

The story seemed to work. Richard Gere was Dixie Dwyer, a struggling cornet player whose future blossoms when he saves legendary gangster Dutch Schultz from a gangland 'hit'. Gregory Hines is Sandman Williams, dancer and gamblers' numbers runner. He wants to be a star and make love to Lonette McKee's Lila Rose Oliver. Meanwhile Dixie has the hots for Diane Lane's Vera Cicero who unhappily belongs to Schultz.

Like Coppola's most famous movies it's all about the family: the white Dwyer family, the black Williams family and the Mob as a family.

Nicolas Cage points out that most of the characters were based on real people. 'I was a guy named Vincent Coll. Mad Mick they called him. So, Mad Dog Dwyer. Me the gangster, my brother Dixie the movie star. The only thing is Mad Mick Coll's brother was a punk named Peter. Dixie Dwyer is class and you don't have to look far past the career of George Raft to see what real-life character inspired the role. That is, to an extent. Everything was "to an extent" in the movie. That's why it's fiction.'

Cage had a strong part in the movie but, like everyone involved, he was bored and rather at sea on the project, which seemed to lack direction. Eventually he lost patience and trashed his trailer, almost destroying it: 'I was very frustrated on *Cotton Club*. I was slated for three weeks' work. I was there for six months, in costume, in make-up, on the set in case Francis got an idea that would involve my character. Meanwhile I'm getting offers of starring roles in other movies and I can't do them. So my behaviour – all the acting out – came from frustration. I was young. I was behaving like a guy who listened to early Who music and wanted to be a rebel, a punk rocker, an outlaw of some sort, and didn't really know how to act. I took a Method approach. I was trying to be like heroes like Robert De Niro. I don't do that now but because I went through that period it still comes back to bite at me sometimes.

'I tried to change my look, walk and my voice – my voice mainly through low self-esteem. I never felt my voice had any character to it so I was always trying to experiment. When you start at an early age and you don't have a lot of experience to draw on, you're sort of put in a position where you've got to try everything – it's part of the experimenting *and* the growing.'

His friend Jim Carrey remembers the wild days: 'At one time Nic was just a little bit dangerous to be around. He was just expressing himself. He'd stare at someone in a really weird way just to see what the reaction was. And I'd say, "Well, what are you being a psycho for?" But he's matured. He's gotten sophisticated about it now.'

Cage recalls: 'I was trying to create a mythology around myself. All my heroes had stories around them, whether they were true or false. I learned that you can't have a life if you live the part but then I *wanted* to generate stories about myself.'

Richard Gere's contract called for him to be paid $125,000 for every week he worked past his contracted wrap-up date of 30 October 1983, on top of his $3 million salary, but *The Cotton Club* problems made him increasingly angry. *The Cotton Club* certainly was not a good experience. 'On paper it all looked wonderful and smooth,' Gere says now.

He is a physically beautiful man who tries to disguise it with spectacles, well-worn sweater, jeans and a retiring attitude. For a couple of decades he has disdained the more obvious trappings of Hollywood glamour in search of a higher plane which he has found in Tibetan Buddhism. Almost every morning he devotes at least forty-five minutes to Zen and Tibetan meditation, which he says helps him become 'very centred and focused'. While most Hollywood headliners concern themselves with fudging time for their private exercise trainers Gere keeps strict priorities and is emphatic: 'Even if I don't really have time I'll just say: "Forget everything else, I'll be late."'

For years he was reluctant to talk at length about his devotion to Buddhism but now – at forty-eight in 1997 – with those shock waves of silver hair the only blatant age indicator, he is less remote and more relaxed about it. When his marriage to Cindy Crawford collapsed, he went to India and Mongolia seeking further spiritual development. He is not shy about his beliefs but guarded. 'I had no interest in talking publicly about my Buddhist practice. It was too important to me, too private. There came a point when His Holiness [the Dalai Lama] said: "We need help." He asked me to do it. Essentially, the gig is to get past the ego – any way you can – to achieve wisdom and compassion and there are incredible levels of that. My ultimate goal is to get rid of all the anger, hatred and jealousy in my life, to become everything I want to be.'

Many of his movie characters or surroundings are seriously warped but he finds no conflict with his spiritual beliefs: 'It's hard for people to understand that acting is just a job. A really good job. It pays really well, gives you lots of opportunities, leisure time, time to think, which is really important. You're not worrying about coming up with a meal or a roof over your head and that's real luxury. I'm able to think about other issues.

'Acting is not a deep, heavy, sacrificial, angst job. There is no dichotomy whatsoever between my philosophy and the characters I play. These things are ancillary. This is just a job, believe it or not.

'It's a job I like a lot but it's not my life. And it never occurs to me for a second that it's really important.

'Buddhism has helped me ease up in my attitude to acting and to the characters I play. Specifically, it has taken some of the pressure off the decision-making process. I could see it as a piece of work. I do the best I can but I don't have to identify so clearly with it. This is not my life. I am not this guy or that guy or any of the characters that I've done that I thought I was so connected to.'

Robert Evans admits he is no angel but he is a Hollywood legend and, if you like characters on the racy side, a naughty delight. Evans's life has been punctuated with pills, cocaine and girls. Lots of girls. And wives. Ironically, he created *The Saint* for the 1997 big screen and even had the audacity to cast 'bad boy' Val Kilmer as his title star.

Evans is Hollywood's greatest lover boy, the man who always put retired Lothario Warren Beatty into second place. As he was walking out of a Beverly Hills restaurant in late 1996, a young woman spotted him. He was wearing his trademark yellow cashmere sweater over an open-necked white dress shirt and is clearly age-challenged. But the Christy Turlington-type admired his straw hat so he gave it to her. 'Keep it,' he said, with his winning grin. She scribbled down her phone number.

'What could I say? I like to be friendly.' Evans smiled in the screening room of his 1910 French Regency estate, which once belonged to Greta Garbo and is a moment's drive from the centre of Beverly Hills and the world in which he has been gambling for four decades. However, things are not always as they seem – especially in Hollywood.

Evans goes on: 'My movies have made billions but you have more in the bank than I have.' You glance around at his surroundings, at the Hockney and Picasso on the walls, and he smiles: 'Thankfully I have friends. Throughout the 1980s I earned about ten thousand dollars and that was from a photograph of me that was used for an advertising campaign. But I picked myself up and I am back in business again. That is what it is all about it – reversing problems rather than immersing in them. God, if I can do it so can everyone else. We can come back even when all around us think we're dead.'

But Robert Evans wasn't just dead. He was buried. After *The Cotton Club* and conviction for possession of cocaine he couldn't even get a coffee at the commissary at Paramount Studios, which he had turned into the number-one studio in the world when as its boss he produced a remarkable series of films including classics like *The Odd Couple* and breakthrough movies like *Goodbye Columbus* as well as *Love Story* and *The Godfather*. 'It was hell. For a decade, for the eighties, I had nothing. I have all this energy and for a whole ten years there was nothing. Wait, that's not true. I had the loyalty of my friends. They helped me survive. Warren and Jack and people like that helped me.'

He shrugs: 'Everything about *The Cotton Club* went wrong. Al Pacino had turned down the lead, Sylvester Stallone took it, and then dropped out and it was eventually a critical and commercial belly-dive flop. It was one of those projects where nothing would go right. I went to people I had made millions for and asked for financial help and these people, men, turned me down. Now, women I knew offered to write cheques just to get me through from Friday to Monday on the payroll. Women are much more loyal. It was an evil and difficult time for me. I thought I could never turn it around. But something makes you go on. I did it. With help from some friends.

'Hollywood is full of stories about movies like *The Cotton Club*. No one said making movies was easy. Or all laughs. But they go on – look at Coppola. He's still making movies. And Nic Cage is a big star now. Richard Gere didn't suffer.'

And after *The Cotton Club* Coppola and his talented nephew stuck together. It was the start of Cage's escape from the Pack.

Chapter Seven
The Gang

'To be a good actor you have
to be something like a criminal.'

Nicolas Cage, 1996.

Nicolas Cage emerged in the Hollywood of the 1980s. That decade set all sorts of records for awful films and huge box office returns, but it was as despised as flared trousers. Of course, the Hollywood value system had not changed: the bottom line was still the dollar. All that was needed were new leading men and women to bring in the audiences and the money.

New faces meant young faces. Nic Cage was one of the crowd – but also apart from it. He was studying wine at the University of California at Los Angeles (UCLA) and was as much into Wagnerian opera as acting.

In the mid 1980s his image resembled that of Marlon Brando in *The Wild One*. Every midnight he was supposed to be roaring along Sunset Boulevard on a high-powered motorcycle, cruising around and making it with chicks. His best buddy was said to be bad-boy actor Mickey Rourke.

Cage cringes. 'That whole motorcycle thing – it's gotten way out of hand.'

Yet there was some truth in it: 'I was feeling restless and I happened to see *Easy Rider* and thought, Yeah, I have to go get a motorcycle. As it happened a lot of other people had the same idea at the same time so I got lumped in with the whole Hollywood motorcycle club.

'I know Mickey Rourke and I like Mickey Rourke but I never once rode motorcycles with him. These stories of us roaring up to after-hour clubs . . . I don't belong to any social clubs.'

But he could do nothing about his membership of the Brat Pack, which seemed to include everyone in Hollywood of a certain age. Some set the running while others followed. Some just hung out and hoped. It was, remembers Cage, a crazy time. He was madcap rather than crazy, intrigued rather than wild. He was always, it seemed, in search of a character. While some of the Packers were out to impress those around them with how cool they were, Cage would wander off at his own quirky tangent: 'I remember one time I went into the Carpeteria [a Californian carpet supermarket] showroom on Vine in Hollywood and made it a point to stay in the store for five hours and talk to all the clerks and carpet salesmen about carpets for as long as I could. I would ask them really stupid questions like: "How is shag made?" or "What colour can I match with this?" By the end of five hours these guys had really started to worry about me but I left before they could kick me out. Nobody saw me do it and I didn't do it to impress anybody. I just did it to see if I could pull it off.'

There were three essential requirements to become a Brat Packer: you had to be young, successful and, of course, bratty.

Times change. Most of the Brat Pack have now hit the big thirty and upwards but are still doing well and have retained that certain attitude to life, which dictates you must always be on the prowl for fun and film roles, and vice versa.

Molly Ringwald was queen of the Brat Pack and launched a generation of wannabes (mouth-to-chin lipstick and orange hair). She is an extraordinary example of the Packers: at eighteen she was an actress who had other teens turning out in herds to see her in films like *Sixteen Candles* and *The Breakfast Club*. For a time no one over thirty knew who she was.

In 1986 she made *Pretty in Pink* starring as the girl from the wrong side of the tracks falling for straight up and downer and Packer alumni Andrew McCarthy. It became a quintessential Brat Pack movie.

In the sixties the Rat Pack – Frank Sinatra, Dean Martin, Peter Lawford, Joey Bishop and Sammy Davis Jr – worked and played together. The eighties equivalent erupted in 1981 with *Taps* as the first Brat Pack movie. Its stars were Timothy Hutton, Sean Penn and

Tom Cruise. It was a critically well-received story about cadets taking control of a military school, although it didn't see much success at the box office. However, it boosted the career of Tom Cruise who, in 1997, with *Jerry Maguire*, set a record of five consecutive films earning more than $100 million. Cruise graduated from *Taps* with *Risky Business, All the Right Moves, Legend, Top Gun*, and *The Colour of Money*, with Oscar-winner Paul Newman, and Oscar-winning picture *Rainman* with Dustin Hoffman. It was *Risky Business*, in which Cruise did his rock 'n' roll performance in Ray-Bans and Y-fronts, that first showcased his appeal to the world.

Sean Penn has not enjoyed such box office success but is still regarded as the 'young De Niro'. Timothy Hutton (back on form as a crime boss in 1997's *Playing God*) is the only Brat with an Oscar (Best Actor in a Supporting Role in 1980's Robert-Redford-directed *Ordinary People*). Rob Lowe, the pretty Packer, has never achieved expectations: his films include Coppola's *The Outsiders, Class, The Hotel New Hampshire* and *St Elmo's Fire*. Judd Nelson, one of the *Breakfast Club* alumni, co-starred in *St Elmo's Fire* and *The Billionaires' Boys Club*.

Matt Dillon started out with S. E. Hinton and Francis Ford Coppola (*The Outsiders, Rumble Fish*) and followed on with *The Flamingo Kid* and *Kansas*. His younger brother, Kevin, starred in *Catholic Boys, The Rescue*, a remake of Steve McQueen's *The Blob* and the Oscar-winning *Platoon*.

Kevin Bacon of *Diner* and *Footloose* is an East Coaster who was in and out of the Pack much like New Yorker Matthew Broderick of *War Games, LadyHawke, Project X, Ferris Bueller's Day Off* and *Biloxi Blues*.

Brat Pack president was Emilio Estevez. The jock in *The Breakfast Club* and the eldest son of Martin Sheen, he was the leader from the start, while making movies like *Repo Man, St Elmo's Fire, That Was Then . . .* and *Wisdom*, which he wrote, directed and in which he starred. Estevez and his brother Charlie Sheen, who starred in the Oscar-heavy *Platoon, Wall Street*, with Oscar winner Michael Douglas, and *Major League*, co-starred together in *Young Guns*, the Brat Pack Western.

As well as Molly Ringwald the ladies of the Pack included Ally Sheedy, who was also a member of *The Breakfast Club* as well as a player in *War Games* and *St Elmo's Fire*.

Laura Dern, daughter of Bruce and actress Diane Ladd, has given performances in non-pack movies like *Smooth Talk* and *Mask*, but she is included as a Pack member because of her role as the girl next door in David Lynch's *Blue Velvet* and her co-starring role as Lulu opposite Nicolas Cage in Lynch's *Wild at Heart*.

Demi Moore was in *Wisdom* and *St Elmo's Fire* before running from the Pack into the arms of Bruce Willis and becoming Hollywood's highest-paid leading lady in 1996's *Striptease*.

Most stunning if not most successful of the ladies was Rebecca de Mornay, who was the call girl in *Risky Business*. She was also *The Slugger's Wife*, but captured more points as a supporting player in Geraldine Page's Oscar-winning *The Trip to Bountiful* and as *The Hand That Rocks the Cradle*.

It was with these young stars that Cage flirted. He watched, he learned and he enjoyed the Pack. But he would as happily 'do a Garbo' – or talk to carpet salesmen – as do the Brat Pack Hollywood Hop. Each night the ritual took place, sometimes with a different cast but the ritual itself remained constant. Cage would either watch it or take part: often it was at the Hard Rock Café off Beverly Boulevard on a Thursday evening. Why Thursday? 'Not a cool night to stay in, man.'

So there they were on a *cool* evening in 1984, the year in which Cage and Sean Penn were *Racing with the Moon*. The boys wore T-shirts, sunglasses and shorts, and the girls wore miniskirts and Madonna hair. Above the blare of rock music, they shouted jokes and stories to one another over cheeseburgers and long-necked bottles of Corona beer. The waitresses smiled and laughed as the boys and girls floated from table to table, partying with a spirit that said they had no responsibility for the next day that could possibly be more important than this night.

At one round table in the middle of the room sat a group of boys who seemed to exude a magnetic force. As they toasted each other and chugged their beers, the prettiest of the girls would find some excuse to walk by the table. They would eye the boys as languorously as they could, hoping for an invitation to join them.

The boys stared back with equal enthusiasm, choosing the prettiest of the pretty and beckoning with smiles. There were many boys in the bar, and many as handsome as those at this one round table, but these boys – the young studs, all under twenty-five, decked out in *Risky Business* sunglasses, trendy sports jackets and designer T-shirts – *they* were the Main Event.

A girl named Alice straightened her long white T-shirt over her blue skirt, brushed her jet-black bangs away from her eyes, patted her hips with her hands and walked slowly to the table. She went to the boy with the firmest chin and the darkest sunglasses. She knew he was Rob Lowe and that he was involved with an actress named Melissa Gilbert, but from the open smile he gave her as she walked over, she felt confident. 'Hi,' she said.

He took her hand and shook it. 'Nice to meet you,' he said.

'My name is Alice,' she said.

He did not tell her his name. He had already turned his head toward a pretty blonde who had just walked by. He flashed her his open smile; she returned it and walked over to the table.

But by the time the blonde girl arrived, Rob Lowe had long since forgotten she was coming. He had turned back to the table, where his friends had once again raised their bottles in a toast: for no reason, the boys were about to link bottle and unite in a private pact, a bond that could not be broken by all the pretty young girls in the room, or even, perhaps, by the other, less famous young actors who shared their table as friends. As the bottles clinked, the boys cried together at the top of their lungs, '*Na zdorovye!*'. Literally it is Russian for 'good health', but for them it was a private signal that only they understood. Afterwards, the boys turned their attention back to Alice and the other girls who surrounded the table and smiled. The girls smiled back.

If Rob Lowe seemed to be inviting all too much attention from the girls, Judd Nelson acted as though he wanted nothing to do with it. His fame, too, attracted them – they recognized his tough-guy looks from his role as the wrong-way kid in *The Breakfast Club* and sought his attention. But, as Alice sat down in an empty chair next to him,

Judd Nelson announced to anyone within earshot, including Alice, 'There is a line. When someone crosses the line, I get angry. And when someone sits down at the table, they have crossed the line.'

Only one of the famous young boys seemed to take the attention in his stride. Emilio Estevez looks like his famous father and his sweet, innocent smile drew still more women to the table. He could not resist them. 'She was a Playmate of the Month,' he whispered, as an exotic-looking woman in a purple jumpsuit took the seat next to him and smiled like an old friend. 'The last time she was here, we were telling her about a friend who had passed the bar exam, and she said, "I didn't know you needed to take a test to become a bartender."' He laughed at her stupidity. But then he turned his attention to her, and before long, the toasts were over. Rob Lowe went home to the girlfriend waiting for him in Malibu. And at 1.35 a.m., after leaving the Hard Rock, calling at a disco and then at an underground punk-rock club, Judd Nelson took off by himself in his black jeep. Emilio Estevez and the Playmate went off together into the night.

The 1980s Brat Pack at play.

Just like Frank Sinatra's Rat Pack they, too, carried their friendships over from life into the movies. They made major movies with big directors, picked up huge contracts, limousines, agents and legions of fans who wrote them letters, bought them drinks, followed them home. And, most important, they were box office. Whenever possible, the Brat Packers acted together – and it would have been surprising if a movie fan had not seen at least one of their ensemble movies. The biggest 'ensemble' with which Nicolas Cage got involved included Sean Penn and Matthew Modine – in different films.

He was of a new generation of actors. His heroes, like Nicholson, De Niro, Pacino, Brando and James Dean, had put in years of acting study. Young actors used to spend years at the knee of such respected teachers as Lee 'Method' Strasberg and Stella Adler before venturing out on stage, let alone into movies. The Cage generation – motto: the magic word is *Now!* – couldn't wait. Not one of the Brat Pack graduated from college: most went straight from high school into acting. On accepting one of his awards for *Leaving Las Vegas* the clearly grateful Cage told the Screen Actors Guild: 'I never went to college. This is my university and I'm gonna consider this award my degree.'

But it was different in the summer of 1984. It was a hot night in Westwood, perfect weather for movie-going, and the leader of the Brats wanted to see *LadyHawke*, which starred Matthew Broderick. But it would not have been cool for a Brat to pay six dollars to the industry that had made him a star. So Emilio Estevez stood outside the Mann's Village Theater, five minutes to show time, considering the various ways in which he might be able to get into the movie free. 'I have a friend who works here who'll get me in free,' Estevez said, but as he eyed the man taking the tickets of the paying customers, he muttered, 'Guess he's not working tonight.' After a moment's thought, he said, 'I could get to a phone, I think I know something I can do.'

With three minutes left, Estevez marched down the nearest street in search of a phone. He peered into a pinball parlour and asked, 'Do they have a phone in here?' They did not. He walked down to a parking lot and heaved a sigh of relief. 'There's a phone,' he said, and trotted off to use it. He called the theatre and explained that he was Emilio Estevez and that the friend who normally let him in free wasn't working tonight; would there be any way to get Estevez passes for the eight o'clock show? Of course, he was told, and when he arrived, the manager and the ticket-taker welcomed him to the theatre and told him how much they loved his movies. 'Thank you,' Estevez said and, with a smile, he dashed off to catch the opening credits.

Estevez, then twenty-three and only five foot six, was already accustomed to privilege and appeared to revel in the attention heaped upon him almost everywhere he went. He has a reputation in Hollywood as a superstud: dozens of girlfriends, many of them groupies, latch on for brief affairs. He was young, single and famous. But the Brat Packers are smart, and Estevez recognizes that with his fame and fortune comes a responsibility to preserve them: he works hard at his profession, building a substantial résumé of acting credits to keep him going. His career began at eighteen, with an afternoon television special, *Seventeen Going on No-Where*. By the time he had

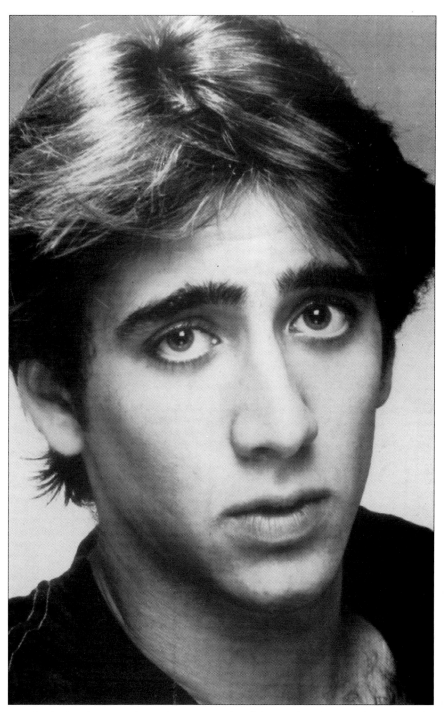

Our fresh-faced Romeo from the wrong side of the tracks who gets the right girl in his early teen hit *Valley Girl*.

Looking for trouble with Vincent Spano, Matt Dillon and Christopher Penn while working for Uncle Francis in *Rumble Fish*.

Where there's a way there's a method – stars Cage and Sean Penn *Racing With The Moon*.

His first big hit out of the cinema ballpark as the emotionally damaged
Vietnam vet in *Birdy*.

In-out-in-out: he made waves as an Olympic oarsman but the movie *The Boy
in Blue* didn't.

Co-star Kathleen Turner hoped he'd die from pneumonia during the filming of *Peggy Sue Got Married*.

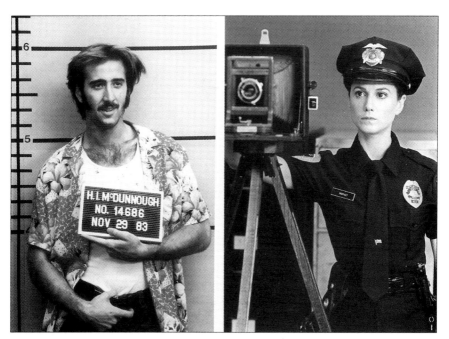

Hi! – you're on police camera. Odd couple thief H.I. McDonnough and his lover cop Holly Hunter in the breakaway comedy *Raising Arizona*.

Dracula lives! Cher brings on the Christopher Lee impersonation in *Moonstruck*.

Is that a snake in your pocket or are you just glad to see me? Laura Dern invest-
igates some Elvis phenomenon in *Wild At Heart* as Sailor weighs-up the cargo.

Gambles that paid off: winning Sarah Jessica Parker in the hilarious *Honeymoon in Vegas* and losing Elizabeth Shue (but getting an Oscar) in *Leaving Las Vegas*.

'Well Stanley, this is another fine mess you've gotten us into'. Sean Connery, with Cage as Stanley Goodspeed, prepare to take on the terrorists in *The Rock*.

The casino is open! Winner takes all. An Oscar in one hand and wife
Patricia Arquette in the other.

made his fourth feature *The Breakfast Club*, he was twenty-one. It was during the filming of *The Breakfast Club* that Estevez became a protégé of one of the most powerful young talents in Hollywood: writer-director-producer John Hughes. Returning to his condo in Malibu after the making of *The Breakfast Club*, Estevez wrote a screenplay called *Clear Intent*. It was surprisingly sophisticated, and when he showed it to Hughes, the reaction was so positive as to assure him a career as a screenwriter.

Clear Intent is the story of two West LA garbagemen who witness a murder and unwittingly get involved. Who will play the garbagemen? 'Maybe Judd Nelson could play one of the parts,' said Estevez one day. Another day he said, 'Boy, I would love to play one of them.' On still another, he asked: 'Do you think Matthew Broderick would be believable as a garbageman?' and then added: 'Sean Penn would be good.'

And what about Nicolas Cage? 'Yeah, I've been thinking about him. He'd be great.' There appeared to be little doubt: *Clear Intent* would unite at least two Brats on screen once again.

One evening the leader of the Brat Pack ordered two slices of pepperoni pizza and a Coke at Lamonica's NY Pizza Stand in Westwood, the home of UCLA and, seemingly, the capital of the generation that buys all the movie tickets. For Emilio Estevez to show his face in this neighbourhood was to invite the stares of countless fans, and as he wolfed down his slices, the rest of the customers watched in silent respect. Moments after he'd sat down, a lanky, greasy-haired young man approached the table. 'Hey, Emilio, how you doin'?'

Estevez looked up expecting to see a fan but the man he saw standing above him was another member of the Brat Pack. Timothy Hutton. 'Hey, Tim, how you doin'?'

'Not bad, man, how you doin'?'

'OK, dude. What are you up to?'

'Not much. How about you?'

'Nothin'.'

Pause.

'You seen Sean?'

'No, I heard he was at the party for Madonna the other night, Sunday or Monday,' Estevez said.

'Oh . . . well, take it easy, dude.'

'OK . . . so long, dude.' Hutton and a small entourage of young men of about his age and greasiness walked back through the pizza joint and into the kitchen.

The Brat Pack whispers that Hutton has made a near-fatal mistake: he has made movies that have failed at the box office.

Another night and the crowds had arrived at the Hard Rock. It was about 11 p.m. and the Brat Pack was in full swing – on their fifth or sixth round of Coronas, and their ninth or tenth round of toasts. The small circle of stars had expanded to include several young actors of their acquaintance, not to mention the dozens of girls who continued to hover near the table.

One young actor was Clayton Rohner. He had most of the credentials necessary to join the Brat Pack: the looks, attitude and presence that suggested acting talent. He seemed especially ebullient – and the reason, no doubt, was that he was celebrating his first starring role in a movie, which might bring him closer to the exalted status of his friends. But the film, *Just One of the Guys*, didn't fit into the same league as *The Breakfast Club*. It was another teen-exploitation flick, perhaps a little better than average, but still not up to par with those of the Brats.

And so, when a young girl of about sixteen approached him with a pen and slip of paper, and asked him for an autograph, Rohner looked immediately at his more famous friends with a sceptical grin. 'One of you put her up to this, right?' he asked. They all smiled and denied it. 'C'mon,' he said, looking at the girl. 'One of these guys told you to do this. Which one? I know one of them did.'

But the girl looked back at Rohner with that special look, the puppy-dog gaze of a fan who has finally come face-to-face with her fantasy. 'Please,' she said, thrusting the piece of paper ever closer to him. He took the pen and, with a flourish, signed his name. Then he looked up again at the members of the Brat Pack. 'I know you guys made her do this,' he said.

But the Brat Packers just shook their heads and watched, without a trace of a smile. Suddenly it was clear that they were as surprised as he was to see the girl leave the table with his autograph, smiling to herself, not bothering to get theirs too.

Fame and fans, especially teenage ones, are fickle.

In 1997 Nicolas Cage is still learning about this although he has been lucky. He attracted an early following, which has grown in size and alongside him in age. He has gone from nerd to cool to lover boy to major character actor and leading man. The constant has always been his image: the bad boy Brat Packer whose family greased his way to fame and fortune. It annoys Cage that no matter what he does – and he can be decidedly eccentric – he cannot lose that public perception of him. 'Maybe it's because I'm not too good at doing the Hollywood thing,' he complained. 'There's a technique involved that I still don't understand, and if you get it wrong you saddle yourself with misconceptions you'll spend years trying to shake.

'I also believe that an actor is someone you see playing a character and there's a danger in revealing too much about your real self because that gets in the way of the illusion you are trying to create on film. I think I'm reticent.'

One producer, trying to conjure up an image for him, suggested: 'Picture Rocky Balboa discussing Dostoevsky – and knowing what he's talking about.'

Actress Maria Conchita Alonso, who has worked with Cage, offers: 'We'd be having a serious conversation and he'd start making these weird faces. Finally, I'd crack up. At first he takes you by surprise but he's extremely generous to work with. And funny. He lives in his own world. You accept it – or you don't.'

Jennifer Beals is also a Cage fan. 'Nicolas would have been a dragon-slayer in another time,' she says, and adds, with a knowing smile, 'He has this struggle for more. To make life more than normal.'

'Sometimes I play games', says Cage. 'I've always thought that things like the devil can't affect me because I don't believe in them. So one night I was talking with a friend and in a cocky way I called up Lucifer and said to my friend, "OK, you can make a deal with him. You can ask for a happy family with love and beautiful children or you can be the next Jimi Hendrix and have three platinum albums and be the guitar revolutionary of the universe." He chose love.

'That night I had a very visceral dream. Some guy that looked like something out of a Dostoevsky novel, with a floppy hat and shabby coat – he looked like Oscar from *The Odd Couple* – walked into the room and all the windows shot up with bricks and I couldn't escape and I felt pure, mortal terror in my heart. He said: " I'm Francisco Durante and I'm the Devil." And he pointed his finger at me and he glared at me and I woke up, terrified.

'The next day I looked up Francisco Durante in the Encyclopaedia Britannica and there was this guy from eighteenth-entury Naples, which is where my family is from, and he was a teacher of classical music. *Strange.*'

Chapter Eight
Smoke Screens

'It was like watching a two-hour car crash.'

Cher, on Nicolas Cage's performance in *Peggy Sue Got Married*, 1986.

I n the spring of 1996 Nicolas Cage and his friend Jim Carrey were
looking for some relaxation in Beverly Hills. The duo wanted some
good wine – and a smoke. Now, smoking, of any variety, within
California's 90210 postal code is frowned on even more than it is in
other places in politically correct America. Which is why they have
'smoking clubs', like the one owned by actor, *bon vivant* and
permanently deeply tanned George Hamilton. Such places have their
customs. Cage feels the need for such ceremony: 'A cigar can be a
good ritual.'

Customers store their cigars at Hamilton's and can call upon the
house brands of wine and tobacco. Cage tells his tale: 'Jim and I went
to George Hamilton's wine bar. He's an interesting one. He was there
and had some fun stories. I told him how he was one of my heroes
from the time he played Evel Knievel. We had cigars and very
expensive bottles of wine were opened and Jim and I were going:
"This is great, man!" At the end of the night we got slapped with an
eight-thousand-dollar bill. It was at that point that George became
the fox in the Pinocchio story. He happens to look quite a bit like that
fox. I would not want to play cards with George Hamilton.'

A decade earlier Cage and Carrey had been locked – 'trapped', they
said – in a long motel stay in Santa Rosa, California. They were both
appearing in Francis Coppola's *Peggy Sue Got Married* – Cage as co-
star, Carrey in a small role. They relieved the monotony by getting up
to all sorts of pranks including luring room service waiters into 'hold-
ups', in which they used prop guns, and the pair established what

appears to be a lifelong friendship. 'Nic is representative of the Picasso form of acting,' says Carrey. 'He doesn't mind putting the two eyes on one side of the face.'

Cage had moved on to *Peggy Sue* after playing it straight as *The Boy in Blue*, which had been intended as a Canadian version of *Rocky*, but centring on rowing rather than boxing. Cage, all tan (unnatural) and muscle (his own), was Ned Hanlan the nineteenth-century smuggler and seaman who became a champion oarsman. The role involved much footage of Cage stripped down – the hunk look that Cage didn't like. And audiences didn't like the film. Cage remains positive about all his work: 'The movies that I made that were mistakes I always learned something from.' But of *The Boy in Blue* he says: 'When I saw that I thought, Well, I'm never going to take my shirt off again – or at least not like that. I wanted to get as far as I could from the beefcake image.'

Well, he did that with Charlie Bodel, his creation for *Peggy Sue Got Married*. He gave Charlie a pompadour with platinum and a squeal of a voice like Minnie Mouse on helium. He was grotesquely over-the-top wonderful. Or dreadful. It all depended on your point of view.

'Everybody wanted him fired,' reports Jim Carrey. 'Francis had the producers up to the house for spaghetti to calm them down.' His Peggy Sue – Kathleen Turner – visited for pasta quite a few times.

'Francis blamed me and he hasn't asked me to work with him since,' says Cage of *Peggy Sue Got Married* which, until *Leaving Las Vegas*, was his most controversial performance. He laughs now about the reaction to the film, which was released in 1986. 'I was reading books about Edvard Munch, about how people were lambasted for their art.'

Cage denies it now but during the filming of *Peggy Sue Got Married* a story circulated that he locked himself in a wardrobe with a copy of Munch's *The Scream* and spent hours staring at the image to prepare himself for the film. Some wags said he was preparing for working with Kathleen Turner. Cage shakes his head now about the Hollywood tale: 'Lock myself in a closet? It's a great story but I don't recall . . .' He continues: 'I welcomed the idea of bad reviews because that would mean I was doing something that would challenge the critics. I thought I could change acting, which isn't really a goal any more. But at the time I was headstrong.'

That was not one of the words his co-star Kathleen Turner used about him. There were plenty of F words, one of which was *fire* him. Uncle Francis remained loyal in the face of her tirades but the pressure on him was just a touch away from intolerable. His nephew argues: 'Francis kept at me to do the picture and he gave me *carte blanche*. Yes, if he had not been directing I would have been fired. It was a weird world. I was twenty-one and it was a time when I was wearing pyjamas to bed so that I could roll out at two a.m. and go to Denny's café and have steak and eggs and roll back into bed. I was bored and I needed distractions so I went to Toys R Us because I never got an E-Z Bake oven as a child. I always thought they were really cool but I don't think my father knew to buy me one because they were sort of for girls – but I wanted one, *deeply*. I thought the way the cakes came out with the chocolate icing looked really tasty. I know people want to connect this with the frustration of working on the movie but I was having a *blast*.

'I'd turned it down four times. Francis convinced me to take it. He said it would be like *Our Town*. He said he really wanted me to be in it. I asked: "If I do, can I change my voice and do something different with it?" He asked: "How different?" I said: "I want to talk like Pokey." Pokey was a character on the *Gumby* show on television and I was channel surfing and I heard that voice. It stuck with me. That's the way my brain works.

'My character was an adult who goes back to high school, to the time in his life when a guy's voice hasn't necessarily changed yet. Also, Francis was doing a story about a woman who goes back in time via her dream. He painted the trees pink and the sidewalk salmon. Why can't actors bend things a little bit too?

'Francis said: "We'll see what happens in rehearsals." So I started doing this way-out voice and people were rolling their eyes and saying, "What the hell is going on?" If anything, Kathleen Turner was frustrated with me. Here she is in this great star vehicle directed by a great director and her leading man comes along with buck teeth and ultra-blond hair talking like Pokey from the *Gumby* show. I can understand why she might get pissed off. Kathleen Turner came over and said, "You know, a film is a permanent record. Be careful what you do."'

Jim Carrey, who had a front-stage seat at the action – and the angst – says: 'When we first hung out he was a little crazy, a little frivolous – raw emotions coming out of everywhere with a lot of anger. He was occasionally embarrassing to be around. Everybody in my life has whispered in my ear at one point, "He has a lot of talent but what the fuck is he *doing?*"'

Diva Kathleen Turner wondered indeed.

For some years she and her husband Jay Weiss were members of an eight-strong rock group called the Favourites ('because we only play our favourite songs') and entertained the crowd at New York's Bitter End Café on Friday evenings. It was all sixties sound: the actress had been a toddler during the fifties when Buddy Holly and the Crickets were chirping around the record charts with hits like 'Peggy Sue'. However, as the star of Coppola's film, which turned out to be his biggest commercial hit since *The Godfather*, she had a leading-lady position to maintain. Tearaway Cage was not someone Central Casting would have sent round to support that image.

Coppola himself replaced Penny Marshall as director and Turner, the biggest female movie star of the decade, took over the Peggy Sue role when Debra Winger dropped out. Somewhat surprisingly, this innocent nostalgia outing fitted her perfectly.

The title wasn't as big a hit with the cinema critics as it had been in the pop charts thirty years earlier, but Turner escaped with her reputation intact and enhanced. It was a girl-next-door-view of an actress who could turn in the screen's sexiest and sultriest performances since Rita Hayworth in *The Lady from Shanghai*.

Peggy Sue Got Married was a female *Back to the Future*. With Buddy Holly in the background we see Peggy Sue in her fifties blue ballgown for her present-day high-school reunion. Then there is a swirl, a collapse and the mother-of-two, about-to-be-divorced Peggy Sue is whisked back twenty-five years into petticoats and pointed bras.

'I don't think I was the most believable teenager,' laughs Turner, who was then thirty-two. She admits that Peggy Sue was very different from the scheming Matty Walker of *Body Heat*, the dress designer/prostitute of Ken Russell's *Crimes of Passion*, Jack Nicholson's Mafia hit-lady lover in *Prizzi's Honour* and even the romantic heroine and Michael Douglas partner of *Romancing the Stone* and *Jewel of the Nile*. 'I mean the girl was so *nice*. Sweetest girl I've ever played. Peggy Sue gets to play with her fate. I just worried about her so much. So nice. It was the first time on screen I haven't had to look gorgeous. I decided I wanted to do it the minute Francis and I took a drive here in Los Angeles and started to sing songs from that era. We had a lot of fun.'

She will still not be drawn into disclosing anything about the behind-the-scenes discussions – Hollywood's polite euphemism for blazing rows – mainly because she found herself in a hit. And an Oscar nomination for Best Actress.

The success of the tale of a woman transported back to 1960 when she was Queen of the Prom and her present-day cheating husband was Prom King, an aspiring pop star – he wants to be Fabian – still seems to amaze all those involved. They talk of star charisma. And star chemistry. But the combination of Turner and Cage seemed more like something for the Bomb Disposal Squad. Yet it took Turner and Cage on to better things. Perhaps it was because they were both their own people.

'When I first read *Peggy Sue* I wasn't interested,' said Cage. 'Then I saw something there – the hopelessness of the situation. I like the idea of someone trying to maintain their dignity with the odds totally against them. Imagine dating someone who knows that you will be divorced twenty years later on. Now, that's really a no-win situation.'

He never thought about the age gap – most of the actors were younger than the actresses at Peggy Sue's class reunion – but concedes that he and Turner had different acting styles. If age came into it at all she was old school.

Turner is, perhaps, her own severest critic: 'To some people I have this image as a very confident, sometimes aloof person who has made brilliant career choices. They should only know the insecurities!' She, and her friends and directors, insist that she is very much more

Peggy Sue than a screen siren. Since 1984 she has been married to real-estate developer Jay Weiss and they have a big town house with a Japanese garden in New York's Greenwich Village, and plans for a family. 'We met when he found me an apartment and to thank him I took him to lunch.

'At two a.m. we were still talking. The chemistry was incredible. Some men back away because they feel I'm too forceful, too independent. Not Jay. He was one of the few men near my age who had such a strong sense of himself he didn't have to incorporate his woman into his identity. But it does disturb him when I do nude love scenes. After all it's hard to act something as basic as sexual excitement without arousing it. I'd be disturbed if he wasn't disturbed.'

Turner is serious, ambitious and, as she says, looking forward to a future of substantial roles. She understands what her image has become but doesn't understand why: 'I never thought of myself as sending out messages, of having the body or personality that sends out certain vibrations. Something must happen in front of the camera that I'm not always aware of. As an actress sensuality and eroticism are tools that I decide consciously to use. I take deliberate actions to push this button, pull that lever, employ a particular voice, to accomplish the seduction of a man. It is a structure approach and is not at all instinctively animalistic.'

She likes to be the centre of attention, which wasn't easy with Nicolas Cage as her co-star. But he says he learned from watching 'a *star*' in action. 'There's a confidence, a way of carrying themselves – you don't get born with it. You acquire it or learn it. Somehow. There's that "it" that they have.'

Of course, he now has that himself but then he was caught up in another star's presence – and dictates. 'I don't think she blamed me after she saw the movie,' says Cage, 'but while we were making it she was: "What are you doing? You're ruining the movie." She was dealing with what? Jerry Lewis on acid? I *was* reading books on Munch then and how everyone hated his works. I thought I had to be met by opposition because I had this arrogant, headstrong attitude at twenty-two. I thought it would be entertaining to everyone then I began to see that it wasn't. I was delighted when I got horrible reviews.'

The strange, nasal whine caused a debate: was Cage wonderfully inventive or simply awful? Some reviews were bad, like 'romantic goofball' (*Cosmopolitan*) and 'miscast' (*New Yorker*) but Richard Corliss (*Time*) was impressed: 'With his dinky voice and fake teeth, professing ardour in a gold lamé jacket or smacking the dumbness out of his forehead, Charlie can endear or exasperate. Cage's brave turn teeters towards caricature, then tiptoes back toward sympathy.' But Cage highlights the negative ones: 'I would have been miserable if I had not gotten bad reviews. I even cut them out. One said I was "a wart on an otherwise beautiful film". Another called me "a poorly wired robot". It was expected. I didn't care. I was happy with the result of the movie. A lot of my friends who didn't like it at first now like it. It did well. Kathleen Turner got an Academy Award nomination and it made a lot of money. But I was lambasted by the critics.

'Francis *did* blame me. He hasn't changed his mind about me. I wanted to be in *The Godfather: Part III*. I thought that I would be a more logical choice as Jimmy Caan's son than Andy Garcia. I would have loved to have been in Francis's *Dracula*.

'Dracula is one of my favourite characters in literature. Much of my life is modelled after him. I just admire the sensibility. The Gothic décor of my homes is inspired by it. To me Dracula is love in exile. I'm very inspired by that idea.

'I don't drink blood but otherwise . . .'

Chapter Nine

Dracula's Lair

'It's mind blowing to me that sex works.' Nicolas Cage,1987.

There's a grand feeling of recklessness about Nicolas Cage, which runs through his life, from his sex games to his real-estate investments, from his humour to his friends. Jim Carrey sticks with him. So does Johnny Depp. He used to go clubbing with Julian Lennon and, in the Brat Pack days, he had a VIP Card to the Hard Rock Café and knew all the stage exits from the Sunset Strip clubs. For a time, the back door of the Playboy Club, just along from Doheny Drive on Sunset Boulevard, was a favourite hang-out.

He has a membership card to the Los Angeles boutique Trashy Lingerie and explains, 'It's for gifts.' The card reads: 'The bearer is entitled to the "privileges" of Trashy Lingerie.' Privileges? 'I have no idea what they are,' says Cage, with a blank expression.

Women have played an important part in his life. The female influence has always been there – in mind and body or both. On film he has worked with strong women – Holly Hunter in *Raising Arizona*, Cher in *Moonstruck*, Kathleen Turner in *Peggy Sue Got Married*, Shirley MacLaine in *Guarding Tess* – and this has worked in his favour. It was a female director, Martha Coolidge, who gave him his big break.

He has been called an 'unlikely' sex symbol but has his own appeal: he is quick, bright – and a rich movie star. He's got heavy eyelids and a voice that always sounds as though he is about to clear his throat. However, it has been his actions rather than his body that have made him stand out. He has a quality that is rare in Hollywood: balls. 'I've never wanted to feel a coward. It's always been important to me to take a fucking chance.'

American *Vogue* called him 'an acquired taste' but Cage has been around long enough to prove that it's a pretty catholic taste. There have been many 'explanations' for his 'tormented soul' early period but he shrugs that off as: 'Hormones'. He says: 'You have to remember I started acting when I was seventeen and the hormones were going crazy. I assumed that if I was an actor I would meet more girls. And I did – and I paid for it. I thought that someone was interested in me – my soul or my thoughts – and I didn't want to admit that it was something else. As I got older and drove the sports car and had the high school Prom Queen those things became boring.

'The Prom Queen is the immigrant's dream – I was always attracted to American symbols like the strong blonde. I wanted the girl I couldn't have. I'm not putting it down, for it doesn't matter what compels you to do or create.

'I've read too many biographies of Tolstoy. He found happiness in the religion of the farmers who were living around him. He felt that was where the truth was. Maybe it is,' Cage adds, with the sad look he wears even when he's happy.

But he's quick not morose. In a magazine interview he was asked about his first sexual experience. He thought the enquiry rather forward. It was rephrased: if you could change one thing about your first sexual experience what would it be?

'I would have taken more time,' replied Cage.

Women, he admits, have confused his emotions. He lived for a time with Jenny Wright, a regular on the American daytime soap opera *General Hospital*, and has dated many others, including Cher and Ami Dolenz, daughter of Monkee Mickey and former *Top of the Pops* presenter Samantha Just. 'My experience is that women are naturally superior to men. They're better at Machiavellian tactics – directing the overall course of a conversation – whereas I basically say anything that comes to mind and don't mind being manipulated and directed.'

There has been sex and love and love and sex, and he never seems sure where the two meet and separate. 'I find women utterly mysterious but I don't like dwelling on it. It all sounds like romantic bullshit. The things that happen between a man and a woman are mysterious. I don't really understand why I am attracted to a woman. Love can do more damage than anger if it goes wrong. Anger passes quickly. Love, when unrequited or ignored, is devastating. However, if it is received and returned it's a magnifying glass to everything that is beautiful in the world.

'It's just so bizarre. It's like – I'm not talking about love and romance, I'm talking about sex – mind-blowing to me that it works. Why do I get turned on by a woman? Why do I experience instinct like that? Even on the simplest level the attraction between the sexes is pretty complex. I've always been a fan of Modigliani paintings. I like long necks. But hate talking about that because ultimately it's an attraction of the soul, if there is such a thing. I also find a sharp sense of humour intoxicating. Sex *is* super important but I can remember being so in love with a person that I wasn't able to have sex because I was paralysed. I couldn't perform on that level.'

Cage says he has not been involved with his co-stars – until a film has finished: 'If I was going to have an affair with a lady I would do it after the shoot. It would be more meaningful if it had nothing to do with the movie. I would get nauseated thinking, Well, we're going to fuck because it's going to help the character. I really don't like working without some attachment to somebody. My relationships have been tumultuous but it's all the trials and tribulations that get me wanting to do something. In fact, it's love that inspires me.'

It's also got him into difficulties. When he was dating model Kristen Zang, the mother of his son Weston, he was in a Hollywood club with Julian Lennon. Someone hit his face. It was record producer Guy Oseary, director of A&R at Madonna's label Maverick Records, a former Zang boyfriend. Cage thought it had been a joke – and then he got angry: 'I started to get up and he walked away. He's a kid, basically. I felt bad for him actually. I know if I do fight I fight to kill. My motto has always been Maximum Violence Immediately. That means pushing the nose into the face or whatever you've got to do. So I don't want to get into a fight.'

It sounds an unlikely scenario for the usually amiable Cage who was always troubled by Sean Penn's fists running into photographers' faces. As he always insists, he would prefer to be moved by love – or work.

Despite his wild and wacky image, though, he likes things to be neat, almost compartmentalized. But he'll happily throw a curve on all the notions: 'I remember I used to be very arrogant. I used to say that when I die it's going to be really messy because I believe in the Japanese Samurai code – the more blood the more nirvana you obtain in the other other life – you would reach a higher state. And so I would try to be some sort of modern Samurai in my thinking and brag that I wanted a car accident, just torn apart all over the street.'

He is perturbed that Japanese novelist – and modern Samurai warrior – Yukio Mishima is considered a failure for lacking purity in his suicide. In the ritual, Mishima performed a perfect hari-kiri sidestroke but was not steadfast on the upward dagger cut. His reputation was diminished. 'Does anybody ever stay focused when they're doing that to themselves?' asks Cage, who keeps a four-foot long Samurai sword – usually sheathed – at the top of a mahogany cabinet in one of the eleven rooms of his Germanic 1920s 'castle'. After living in a series of Hollywood apartments Cage decided one evening in 1988 to go out the next day 'and get myself a place'. He did just that.

It is a startling structure, fabulously fake, with battlements and turrets and two seemingly endless staircases. ('I got a really good price on it – *nobody* wants to live in a castle.') Cage's character in *Vampire's Kiss* was called Peter Loew and mail would arrive at the castle for a former tenant, a Peter Laslow. 'That's another of those little tears in the envelope of space and time that I don't know how to deal with and I'm not going to address too much,' says Cage, who is feudally protective of his real estate.

His castle, on a third of an acre high on Loz Feliz in the heart of the Hollywood Hills, was listed on the market for $1,695,000 but through Dorothy Carter and Hodi Hodges of Douglas Properties he bought the 5,367-square-foot house for $1. 5 million. It had been built in 1928 but was gutted and refurbished in 1986. There are three bathrooms, four bedrooms and a maid's quarters. It is on a gated promontory with a 360-degree view of Los Angeles – from the master suite, which has a black marble fireplace, you can see out to the Pacific from the white tile bath.

In the garage is a silver Peugeot convertible, which once belonged to the late Dean Martin. Usually in the driveway is Cage's black Porsche or 1967 metallic blue Corvette Stingray coupé. He also owns a Lamborghini, a Ferrari, a 1967 black-on-black Chevelle, and a Bentley. 'I think of handmade cars as art, as moving sculptures. There is nothing like an Italian car. I have a lot of Italian furniture, I love Italian wine, I love Italian clothes. Forget the fashion or status crap – I don't buy into that. But I think there's an incredible amount of creativity coming out of that country.

'They say there are three ways that God shows himself to us: through the birth of a child, the discovery of true love and the creation of a work of art. Some cars are works of art. The Lamborghini is like a triple espresso. It's like a bull, which is its symbol. You can't go anywhere without the police stopping you. They'll stop you just because you're in that car. They'll stop you even when you aren't moving. I rarely drive – only late at night.

'At least I admit I like these things. These actors work all their lives and start to make money and say, "I'm not really into it, the money's no big deal." I think of the guy who's out there struggling for his next dime listening to the actor saying his millions are no big deal and the guy says, "Fuck you."

Cage has no qualms about spending – showing that purchasing power is a big deal to him. At Easter in 1997 he paid almost half a million dollars at a Geneva auction for a rare 1971 Lamborghini Miura SVJ owned by the estate of the last Shah of Iran. It was the first of four SVJs built and had been driven only 1,897 miles. In the auction, held by London-based Brooks Europe, Cage paid $446,820 (almost double the pre-sale estimated value of the car) following a bid by telephone from California. The 'metallic burgundy' painted car was the most expensive sold in auction in Europe in the first half of 1997.

'I admit I like having the ability to buy these cars. The money also allows me to make low-budget movies for no pay and it may allow me to branch out and try other things. I want to make my own car –

design one.'

All around the castle – and his twelfth-floor penthouse suite, which is home-away-from-home and office near the Grand Central Market in the predominantly Latin section of Los Angeles ('I can imagine I'm in South America or somewhere') – are prizes: pieces that fascinate him, tickle his wonderment. He calls the interior decoration of his castle 'Gothic hot-rod'. He explains: 'It's the sort of feeling I've always admired since I saw Jean Cocteau's *Beauty and the Beast*. That was my dream as a child, to live in the Beast's castle.'

There is a butterfly collection, antler chandeliers, a rosy-red grand piano and carved gargoyles, mixed with sculptures of comic book villains. Above the fireplace, in the main room, is a six-foot metal fly sharing space with a painting of a Hindu princess by Robert Williams. The living room walls are heavy with maroon brocade and in one corner there is a stuffed black beetle which was used in the television science fiction series *Outer Limits*. ('I *had* to have it.')

Gwendolyn didn't make it up the staircase. Cage is interested in martial arts and some confusion resulted from this as to Gwendolyn's identity. In the television series *Kung Fu* which starred David Carradine, the young protagonist was known affectionately as 'grasshopper'. So everyone believed it was a grasshopper that Cage had snared on a Canadian location and with which he returned to Los Angeles. Not so, he says. 'It was a praying mantis. Her name was Gwendolyn and she used to sit on my finger and I'd take her up to flies and wasps and she'd just pluck 'em out of the air and eat them. I don't know if she had any awareness of me but we seemed to have a relationship. Praying mantises don't bother me – you can see the pupils in their eyes and they're very intelligent-looking for a bug.'

He admits he sometimes finds it easier to get along with bugs than with people: 'It's difficult for me to make friends. There aren't too many people I feel comfortable with right away. I met Johnny Depp playing Monopoly in a club. I'd been seeing his ex-girlfriend. At first we didn't like each other but then we did. I told him he should be an actor and he said, "No, I can't act." He could. He did. And the rest is history. But I do find it difficult to get along with other people. Not many are from the same tribe as me.'

Jim Carrey has proved faithful since the madcap *Peggy Sue Got Married* days and success has not changed their relationship. In 1996 Cage got his Oscar and Carrey was the number-two box-office star, after Tom Cruise, in the world. 'Nic and I just hit it off from the start,' says Carrey. 'We come from different worlds but we seem to see things the same way. Nic says that by believing in your own instincts you can leave something permanent behind. I think that too. It doesn't have to be all about box-office statistics.'

Cage tells of the time he and Carrey were driving from Los Angeles to San Francisco. They wanted to find a game to pass the time and settled on naming different kinds of pastries: Ding Dongs, Twinkies, Zingers, Winchell's Maple Bars . . .

Now, now, said Carrey, Winchell's have doughnuts not maple bars. 'I told him, "Yes, there are *bars*." He says, "No." So I said, "Open the Casino."'

This is Cage-speak for gambling. 'Open the Casino' can involve everything from million dollar deals to well, doughnuts. 'Jim suggested betting his guitar for my leather jacket. I wanted higher stakes. I offered a lithograph by Marc Chagall for a neon sculpture of his. We placed the bet and drove into a town, looking for a Winchell's Donuts. I was getting edgy. He was playing on me, saying there was no maple Winchell's *bar*. Then we saw a big yellow Winchell's sign. I got right in there and got up to the counter, took a breath, and asked, 'Can I have a maple bar, please? The guy answers, "Yes."

'So, I won this priceless sculpture and it cost twenty-five cents for the maple bar. It was fun.'

Of course, opening the Casino is always fun – especially if you are Nicolas Cage and you haven't a clue about the odds.

Chapter Ten

Raising the Odds

'It was easy for me to work in the desert because my father was a lizard and mother is a coyote.'

Nicolas Cage, 1987.

Edgar Allan Poe would have loved Nicolas Cage. The Coen brothers did – eventually. Joel, who directs and writes, and Ethan, who writes and produces, created 1987's *Raising Arizona* two years after making their cult success *Blood Simple*.

The brothers – Oscar contenders in 1997 with *Fargo* – took a warped but warm look at domestic bliss. Cage, whom they dismissed at first as 'too urban', finally won the role of H. I. McDonnough, who marries a barren policewoman named Edwina – brought marvellously to life by Holly Hunter. Edwina wants a baby and Hi gets her one. Nathan Arizona just happens to be the heir to a business tycoon . . .

Cage, of course, loved Hi, a mush-head with a penchant for robbing fast-food stores and getting caught. Edwina was his arresting officer. The Coens' dark, offbeat humour seemed a perfect foil for Cage, John *Roseanne* Goodman and award-winning co-star Frances McDormand.

It was a long location in Scottsdale, Arizona, but that was of no concern to Cage. He was in a tremendously focused phase. People would ask him what was bothering him – which irritated him. 'I wasn't upset about anything. I was just concentrating. Now, when something broke my concentration that's when I did get a little upset.'

You can go stir-crazy in the wide-open spaces.

According to 1997 *Fargo* Oscar winner Frances McDormand, Scottsdale was like a big golf course and the nearby desert, though magnificent, not a great distraction. It got off to a bad start for Cage:

his name was misspelled on his canvas chair. Later, a Band-Aid separated 'Nic' from 'olas', the offending 'h' obscured.

He arrived on the set with lots of ideas. Even in an uncomplicated supermarket chase, he proposed a glance at his watch during a lull in the action but Joel Coen politely rejected the suggestion. Their relationship was bumpy but respectful. Cage praised the brilliant script and the Coens' professionalism but would have liked to have been more involved in the production: 'Joel and Ethan have a very strong vision and I learned how difficult it is for them to accept another artist's vision. They have an autocratic nature. With relatively new directors, that's when you find that insecurity. The more movies they make, the more they'll lighten up. The important thing is not to discourage an actor's creative flow.'

Holly Hunter, a friend of the Coens, insisted that she always held the reins, but could rely on Joel as a safety net. 'Joel and Ethan function without their egos,' she says. 'Or maybe their egos are so big they're completely secure with anybody who disagrees with them. I found the best thing to do was bring up your point, drop it, and wait a couple of days.'

Joel Coen knew exactly what the movie was about – and what he wanted from his stars. 'It was a sort of love story that lets us examine the question of parenting. It had all the basic elements of popular contemporary moviemaking – babies, Harley Davidsons and high explosives.' It was totally the opposite of *Blood Simple*. 'We didn't want to do another scary movie. We'd already gotten that out of our system. Also, *Blood Simple* was slow and deliberate. We wanted to try something with a faster pace and a lighter tone. We were ready to do something different. The movie was about parenting, and neither of us was a parent but we're not really intimately acquainted with murder either, and we made a movie about killing people.

'But as with all movies the casting is important – they're the people who have to make it work. Nic was perfect. Hi is a thinker. He struggles with the grand issues. He just has an irrepressible urge to hold up convenience stores. The character is caught in an internal struggle. He's being torn in two different directions. On the one side is his desire to settle down and have a family. On the other side is his inclination to respond to the call of the wild.'

Cage says of Hi: 'What I liked best about this character was his humility. He was a very unusual guy. He played by his own rules but had a lot of integrity. The first contact I had with the film was through the script and I was sold as soon as I read it. I was impressed with it because it required no adjustments. It was terrific to finally find one like that.'

It was clearly a relief for Cage to have moved on to *Raising Arizona* from his crazy Charlie in *Peggy Sue*. It was clear that the Coens were never going to be as indulgent as Uncle Francis. And that *some* lessons had been learned from the *Peggy Sue* débâcle: 'We were all just trying to make the most out of what's on paper. We didn't do a lot of improvisation. Sometimes when you improvise it seems funny at first but in the overview it's only distracting. On *Raising Arizona* we hardly did any improvisation because the screenplay was so reliable.'

Cage's co-star Holly Hunter liked the scrupulously honest but maternally obsessed Edwina. 'We knew Holly as a friend, and we'd seen a lot of her work,' says Ethan. 'We were really impressed with her as an actress, and personality-wise, we were always intrigued by what she seemed capable of projecting.'

'She seemed the type of actor and personality who could convey an unstoppable, brook-no-opposition desire to accomplish something,' said Joel. 'It was that kind of energy that made us think she'd be perfect for this character. When we were writing the part we were sort of hearing her voice.'

The Coens and Hunter met when she was performing on Broadway in the Beth Henley comedy-drama *Crimes of the Heart*. At that time they were casting for the female lead in *Blood Simple*. Hunter was preparing to do another Henley play on Broadway (*The Wake of Jamey Foster*), and so was unavailable for *Blood Simple*. But as the Coens began work on the screenplay for *Raising Arizona* they kept coming back to Hunter as the prototype for Edwina. The part was hers from the time it first appeared on paper.

'Ed's a real straight-arrow kind of woman,' Hunter said. 'She comes from a long line of police officers and takes pride in that militaristic discipline that cops have. In that way, it makes perfect sense that she'd fall in love with Hi because, even though he's an ex-con, he doesn't play games. He comes in and tells her how he feels. She likes men who are straightforward.

'She also has an incredible maternal instinct – a desperate, abnormal, compulsive desire to have a child. It's bigger than anything she's ever confronted in her life.'

The love between the two characters was treated with sympathy and respect. Cage believes that that was the story's comic strength: 'I don't find gag lines particularly funny. Humour has to come out of the attitudes of the characters. This script was funny because you could see something very human in the way these people think and behave.'

Cage's incorrigible H. I. McDonnough makes Nathan Arizona Jr the most celebrated of the much-heralded Arizona quintuplets – heirs to the fortune of furniture tycoon Nathan Arizona. An open casting call was attended by more than four hundred babies to determine who would star as Nathan Jr. Fourteen others also appeared in the film.

All fifteen were used in one scene – in three shifts of five – when Cage, as Hi, is driven to distraction trying to pick a kidnap victim from Harry, Barry, Larry, Garry and Nathan Junior Arizona. It's the movie's big moment.

Cage says he learned much from Holly Hunter. There was lots of time to talk on location – and on film together. And with the babies. Hunter is a strong, individual character: like Cage, she has always walked her own road. Of all his early co-stars she was the most compatible. And in 1987 neither of them had any idea that, not too many years later, they would win Oscars, would be big.

The same year she made *Raising Arizona*, the diminutive actress was nominated for her first Oscar. She and Cage had talked of such moments: 'You discuss your ideas, your dreams – we were both at the start back then.'

Holly Hunter is five foot two, and packed with determination. She enjoys a joke: 'I think I have a good sense of humour but I'm not funny. I'm not like a stand-up comedienne at all. I don't tell a good joke. I don't keep people holding sides.' She talks in a hoarse,

Southern-fried twang: 'I hate being imitated. I'm imitated all the time. "HiiiHolleh howrya doin?" Oooh, that's not how I sound. I know I have an accent. I'm very aware of that . . .

'My comedy comes from a very serious place. It's a matter of being in grave circumstances and taking it very seriously or having something truly at stake that I think makes things funny.'

Working with Cage was her first 'movie-star experience' and *Raising Arizona* her first major film. She won plaudits and so did Cage. Pauline Kael of the *New Yorker* hailed his performance: 'Cage has sometimes been expected to carry roles that he wasn't ready for but his youth works for him here.'

Holly Hunter found working with the babies easier than working with adults: 'We had a couple of baby wranglers that were really great. I certainly did love the baby who was Nathan Jr. He was a fascinating child, and brought a real human aspect to doing the movie. It wasn't like being on other sets, because there was a baby involved and he had no respect for the camera. He had no awareness of meal penalties or overtime. If he didn't feel like doing a scene, then we had to wait and have him take a nap.

'We were constantly aware we were making a movie. It was not brain surgery. It was not real life. It was a movie. Joel and Ethan are very much that way. This was a movie movie. It's a very self-conscious movie and I think they're very self-conscious movie makers. I love that. *Raising Arizona* is not a film. It's a movie. *Out of Africa* is a film. Let's be serious here. It ain't a middle-of-the-road movie. It's made by extremists.'

Extremism is her style. She is of the serious mainstream of Hollywood leading ladies – there's just a handful, including Meryl Streep, Glenn Close and Jessica Lange – but what separates Holly Hunter from that élite group is not that she takes risks but that she *needs* them. It is, she says, what makes her tick.

And the biggest gamble – she calls it a challenge – of her distinguished career so far was the disturbing *Crash* which provoked division and derision from the moment it was unveiled at the 1996 Cannes Film Festival. Film-maker David Cronenberg's excursion into a world of twisted sexuality was called both a masterpiece *and* a dangerous piece of filth which should be banned from cinema screens.

Like Hollywood's other serious leading ladies Hunter bemoans the material on offer as a way of explaining the temptation to make a film like *Crash*. Shaking her head she said: 'You want to do something that is important or daring but the scripts that come through still astonish me. I can't believe they are written. It's almost the year 2000 and I'm still a love interest in many of these scripts. It is so intricately woven into our culture and most movies are just a mirror image of that. Do you wonder that I want to do something different? I admire Meryl Streep. Her women may be obsessed with a man but they are also obsessed with something else, some other aspect of life. There's something considered unattractive about women being obsessed. It's masculine. Generally, women who have the smarts in movies are portrayed as wily, catty and cunning. If they have power, it's sexual power.

'I am willing to explore all of that . . .'

In 1987, Nicolas Cage was still beginning his journey of exploration. With one of Hollywood's most powerful and dynamic women.

Chapter Eleven

Lovestruck

'I happen to think crazy people
make good actors.' Cher.

n 1987, the unpredictable Nicolas Cage was on an unpredictable roll. The admired and respected director Norman Jewison – responsible for such landmark films as *In the Heat of the Night, The Cincinnati Kid* and *The Russians Are Coming, The Russians Are Coming* – was casting his romantic comedy *Moonstruck*.

Cher had signed on as the thirty-eight-year-old widow who decides to remarry only to fall in love with her fiancé's brother, the lovestruck Ronny Cammareri. Who would play Ronny, the baker boy with the wooden hand?

Step forward that funny-voiced actor from *Peggy Sue Got Married*. Cher watched Cage in that film when she was recovering from a car accident and was 'enchanted'. He was, she says, what hooked her into and kept her with the film. 'When we were looking for Ronny it just seemed natural to me that Nicky should play the part. He *was* Ronny. I didn't see that there could be any problems . . .'

There were. The moneymen were not convinced that Cage had the leading-man stature either to help carry the film or believably to sweep Cher's frumpy Loretta Castorini off her feet.

Cher, however, had just made *The Witches of Eastwick* with Jack Nicholson, Michelle Pfeiffer and Susan Sarandon. It had been a long, difficult film with casting problems and Cher was determined there would be no such difficulties on *Moonstruck*. She was the star and she wanted *her* way. And 'Nicky' Cage was what she wanted. When the producers continued to go against her wishes she went on strike for twenty-four hours. A day later, Cage was in. 'She was amazing. She saw something that others didn't in *Peggy Sue Got Married* – you wouldn't think a guy acting like Jerry Lewis on acid was a romantic, powerful lead but she did. She said my performance was like watching a two-hour car accident.

'Cher was a real champion for me. I didn't want to do the movie at first. I wanted to do some punk movie, some wild, rebellious gesture. It's only now that I look back and realize how lucky I was. I don't think I was mature enough to know it or tell anybody that at the time. The film was my first blockbuster.'

Despite Cher's endorsement, he had to do a screen test for the film studio and explains: 'MGM wanted to make sure I hadn't been to the imaginarium too many times. When I say imaginarium I mean a place where ideas have feathers on them. They wanted to make sure I wasn't going to turn the part into something that wasn't on the paper.'

His early reluctance soon turned to excitement. He recalled having watched, as a couch-potato youngster, *The Sonny and Cher Show*, which had been fabulously popular on American television. Then, it hadn't been so much Cher as her partner who had impressed Cage. Or part of him at least: 'I liked Sonny Bono a lot. I liked his moustache. Part of the reason I wanted to have a moustache since I was seven years old is because of Sonny's moustache.'

By *Moonstruck*, Sonny – and the moustache – were out of the picture, which was fine for Cage was all grown-up and ready for Cher: 'It was all so remarkable. God, I was starring opposite Cher. I was twenty-three and doing romantic scenes with her. I was about the same age as Eric Stoltz who played her son in *Mask*. There was an incredible pressure to have a certain amount of male power with her. I remember thinking, I'm going to imagine what it will be like to kiss her.

'When we did kiss there was a lot of power there. She's a passionate woman and I didn't want to kiss her until the time I had to kiss her in the film. And it really worked. It was exciting. I put every thought I had about it into it.'

Whatever he says about 'waiting for the kiss', rumours of a blazing affair between the two went on throughout filming – Cher has a long history of 'toy boys', who include Tom Cruise and Val Kilmer – but Cage is quite reticent about it. Once when asked, point-blank, what Cher was like in bed, he mumbled: 'Uh-oh, wow. Cherilyn. Well, there's – I mean, are you talking about the visual image? I'm sure she's great.'

He is more open about another aspect of Cher: her ego. 'My only disappointment with *Moonstruck* was that some of my best work was cut by the director. Norman Jewison took me out to dinner afterward and said he had to cut some of the scenes because they overshadowed the star.'

Cage's performance as the brooding baker remains a significant achievement. He understands the value of working with Jewison, who has guided so many major talents, and Cher, who had *lots* of stories about his hero Jack Nicholson. Cher remains fond of Cage: 'None of us is one thing – or the one thing that the press picks up. If anyone is a rounded person, Nicky is. To me, Nicky is a Renaissance man. A couple of times I made lunch for Nicky at my apartment. One time he asked me if I was a witch – he was into that stuff – so I said, "I am." He said: "I thought so."'

Cage 'flies' at night: 'I'm better then. The air is cooler and it's cleaner and there's less traffic. But I'm trying to worship the sun and the moon together and not be unbalanced. I can pretty much say that my vampire years are coming to an end.'

Instead, he's into trains. It's just an extension of his childhood. He knows a Raymond Loewy model train from a Dinky toy: 'One of the fondest memories I have of my father is when I was about a year old and he was playing with *his* train set while holding me in his arms. Well, now I'm obsessed with trains. I can't get enough of them. I've amassed a fairly large collection of different scales and sizes of trains. When I told my father about it he came up with a great idea. He suggested I put a loop on the train's sound system so as it goes around the track it says, "Who, why, when, where. . . who, why, when, where . . ." Over and over. He said I could call it the Zen train.'

On *Moonstruck* Norman Jewison was always in charge of the tracks. A blow-up of a radiant Judy Garland stares over his shoulder, and Jewison, director and gentleman farmer, says, 'What draws me to a story is something to do with betrayal. I'm a political person, and power corrupts – it breeds the thousand small betrayals that people live with every day.' His *Moonstruck* is an old-fashioned tale of Italian-Americans in Brooklyn, an adult tale, a corny tale: even the moon does exactly what it should do. Jewison is one of the last realists: 'When people say, "Is your picture going to be a hit?" I shrug. No one knows. If you *knew*, you'd do it every time, but there'd be no secret, there'd be no magic, there'd be no *risk*.'

There was certainly risk in his vision of John Patrick Shanley's screenplay. 'I thought that maybe I could do an opera,' says the director of *Fiddler on the Roof* and *Jesus Christ, Superstar*. 'I think that film is at its most powerful when you're watching something and it's *scored* to some kind of musical expression.' Cher would be his lyric soprano; Cage his tenor; Olympia Dukakis, as Cher's mother, could be the contralto; and Danny Aiello, the fiancé, the baritone; Vincent Gardenia, Cher's father, the bass.

'We'd bring them together and each would have their own wonderful aria. Each would get the chance to say what they feel about the others in their own lives and relationships. We'd bring them together in a fugue and let it build, build, build,' Jewison says, conducting with his hands. 'To a *crescendo*. It would end in a classic way. And if I could weave *La Bohème* through that, maybe we'd have an interesting style. And I'd have an interesting film.'

Moonstruck hadn't been the film Jewison had wanted to make. He had aspired to remake the 1937 British fantasy *The Man Who Could Work Miracles* from a story by H. G. Wells and had spent a year on it when boardroom shuffles killed the project. He was spinning his wheels when MGM sent him *Moonstruck*.

'It came in with the title *The Bridge and the Wolf* and a lot of people thought it was a horror movie. I read it and something happened. First, after all that frustration, I was in the mood for a romantic comedy. Second, I identified with all the small betrayals in the family. That's the strongest relationships you'll ever be involved in, and it *still* happens. It does.'

Jewison liked the *Moonstruck* script. 'He [Shanley] writes about blue-collar people on the streets and uses their dialogue, their passion and makes them bigger than life. Maybe it comes from writing for the theatre or something – it's like he's the Clifford Odets of our time, a playwright driven by ideas.

'Feature films are the literature of this generation and that brings more responsibility to those who make them. It disturbs me when I see film moving into an anti-intellectual area – pure escapism, endless, mindless reels of endless, mindless action. There's nothing wrong with making money, and my greatest fear in life would be to bore somebody in a film. But, that said, unless you've got some ideas behind the story you're telling, why tell the story?'

For Cage the timing could not have been better. He had come off one high profile film, with a strong leading actress, and was in another. He was also working with an ensemble of brilliant actors. He says he began to understand his opportunity as production went on.

It is part of Cage's character that he soaks up experiences and he – and Cher, whose acting credits were slight compared to some of the cast – had plenty in the film about the young widow whose life suddenly changes under the spell of an extraordinary full moon. The two stars were up against Vincent Gardenia, Julie Bovasso, Danny Aiello, Louis Guss, Feodor Chaliapin and, especially, Olympia Dukakis.

If ever two women knew who they were, it's Loretta (Cher) and Rose Castorini (Dukakis), a mother and daughter with a devastatingly attractive certainty about them. Rose's might also be termed dread: she's positive that her husband Cosmo (Gardenia) is stepping out on her. Loretta, who goes around her Italian-accented neighbourhood doing taxes and book-keeping, combines the qualities of a mother, an executive secretary and a great beauty. But as a childless woman, whose husband has been dead seven years, she downplays her every asset mightily. As the film begins she becomes engaged to Johnny Cammareri (Aiello) but it is soon clear that Mr. Johnny hasn't a romantic – or an impetuous – cell in his body.

Before he takes off to the bedside of his dying mother in Palermo, Mr. Johnny has only one crucial request: that his new fiancée look up his younger brother, Ronny. But even before the audience discover that Nicolas Cage is the impassioned baker Ronny, it is evident that

Mr. Johnny had better not hang around in Palermo.

Musically, *Moonstruck* was built around *La Bohème*, whose themes we see and hear at every turn. The lupine Ronny's more civilized side is his passion for grand opera and, in the movie's great Cinderella moment, he lures Loretta to see it at the Met.

The movie impressed the critics, including Richard Natale of the *Los Angeles Herald Examiner*:

> Cage attacks the role of Ronny with a nice balance between unbridled romanticism and tongue-in-cheek seriousness; he's marvellous. Everyone is, yet Olympia Dukakis seems to have an extra sheen of maturity and wisdom that moves her work from authoritative into memorable.
>
> The production itself is a joy, from the photography of David Watkin, who seems to give every scene its own magical glow, to Philip Rosenberg's fine production design, Lou Lombardo's crisp editing and the costumes of Theoni Aldredge, perfect, right down to Cher's ruby slippers, which carry their own movie memories. And whether it came from the editor, director or writer, that shimmering dissolve from the moon itself to the lights of Mr Johnny's approaching plane is what the craft of movie-making is all about.

Cage – despite his cutting-room-floor complaints – got some great scenes and lines: 'Love doesn't make things nice, it ruins everything, it breaks your heart, it makes things a mess. We're not here to make things perfect. The stars are perfect. Not us. Not us! We are here to ruin ourselves and love the wrong people and die!'

Cher says that although she never felt like fleeing *Moonstruck*, she was wary of confronting it. 'Having such a cast and getting Nicky as Ronny helped my confidence but I was frightened of betraying audiences, not delivering what they expected from me. As much as I liked it, it wasn't like *Mask* which I felt I just *had* to do. I was a little frightened because there seemed to be all kinds of possibilities and all kinds of risks here. I wondered if at that point in my career when there might be some people out there interested in seeing my movies they would accept me in the role.'

Dowdy and prematurely grey, Loretta was not Cher the sex symbol: 'She wants to have children but has little time left to do that. So does she marry someone for whom she feels no passion but who will fulfil that wish? Or does she hold out for the right man and perhaps risk not fulfilling that wish? Loretta decides not to wait – but just as she becomes engaged, the right man comes along. All this, of course, causes her an agony of indecision and guilt as well as giving her a sense of freedom.

'But I much preferred playing her "before" than "after". The freedom is not interesting to me because that's something I know, usually. Yet I didn't think of her as being constrained, exactly. My idea was to play her more as bossy and controlled.

'I don't know where I get these ideas but I usually have one for each scene, and if it's right, if it works well, it ends up carrying the whole scene. We all talked about it – someone like Nicky wants to know everything you think, he likes to be involved in the whole experience. It's why, why, why? He's always going to be like that. It's his nature. He's someone who has to know. I like that. I'm the same, really.

'I happen to think crazy people make good actors because they can suspend their belief systems so easily – and making movies you have to go in and out of different realities very quickly. But if everyone was like me, if everyone did what they wanted, who would there be to work the toll booths?

'Nicky is like me. We're a breed apart.'

Jewison says: 'Cher and I both admired Nicolas's work in *Peggy Sue Got Married* but the main reason she felt he was right for the part was because, like the character of Ronny, Nicolas struck her as a tormented soul.'

Cage reflects: 'I was attracted to the romantic element in *Moonstruck* because I think I am a romantic. There haven't been that many great romantic films – *The Graduate* and *Wuthering Heights* come to mind – and I think we need more of them. Even though romance isn't always a fun thing to go through, the things men and women experience through each other are utterly mystical and elusive. Ultimately, *Moonstruck* was a happy family film for an ensemble of actors rather than a purely romantic movie and I think it frustrated Norman that I leant towards interpreting it as a desperately romantic *Beauty and the Beast* fable.

'I didn't change my character from the way it was written, but I did try to play up the wolfish part of Ronnie's personality.'

Jewison concurs: 'Nicolas did have a darker interpretation of Ronny than I did, but we both agreed that a poetic quality was central to the character. When Ronny is first introduced in the film he's in a basement slaving over hot ovens and he almost has the quality of a young Lord Byron.

'Then, as the film progresses Nicolas blossoms into a classic romantic leading man – and I think it was the first film where he'd come off that way. There's one sequence in particular that's a sort of blue-collar re-creation of Romeo and Juliet's balcony scene where Nicolas had the gangling, vulnerable appeal of a young Jimmy Stewart.

'I didn't know then if Nicky would ever be a huge mainstream actor because he took unbelievable chances as an actor. Every time I got angry with him I'd just look in his eyes. In fact, I don't think I saw any other part of Nicky except his eyes because that's what I liked about him. But he did take unbelievable chances. You knew he would be willing to give anything and everything a chance, in love and work – in anything. He was a gambler.'

Which is how he met his wife.

And played a vampire. And ate a live cockroach.

Chapter Twelve

True Romance

'It's safer to be scared than loved.' Machiavelli.

Nicolas Cage was twenty-three and a major movie star. Off-screen he was still acting like a punk. Image was everything, he thought. In fact, in Hollywood it is perception that matters. It is a town in which careers can soar or fall on a chance remark or a wrong gesture. It often doesn't matter who you are but who people think you are.

As a youthful millionaire, Cage wanted the trappings but he also wanted to be *cool*. Part of that was his constant questioning – a habit that irritated Jim Carrey: 'He doesn't just pick up a wedge of cheese. He wants to know the history. He wants to know exactly who made the cheese.'

He was full of illusions and recalls some bad moments: 'I once saw Iggy Pop at a strip club wearing a gold Rolex. There he was, one of my idols – he was such a rebel and explorer – wearing a gold Rolex and I thought it was a statement like, "I can walk in your world but maybe you can't walk in mine." It's like Pete Townsend driving a Lincoln Continental when he was smashing guitars. He was driving the car his parents were supposed to be driving.'

Cage says he has matured in attitude and action: 'I've stopped with the grand gestures. I've learned patience instead of persistence,' but he doesn't sound as if he believes himself. In 1987 he was still researching the history of cheese, always wanting to know who made it.

It was a question he could relevantly ask at Canter's deli in Los Angeles. A popular Brat Pack hang-out, a coffee shop and club to the aspiring in Hollywood, Cage liked it because it had good parking spaces. The Harley or the convertible could easily be on show. It was at Canter's that he went wild one evening, throwing a tomato ketchup bottle at a wall. Joanna Horsley was there that evening and said: 'The place just went silent. Nic was with some girl and kinda swaggering around a bit. It seemed a bit excessive – the management didn't like it. They were very conscious that it was a young person's place. They didn't want trouble with the authorities. Nic just seemed to lose it.'

The Heinz-style hitman smiles shyly about the incident now. He had been young, impulsive. 'I was with a girl that I liked who was older and trying to get me to watch movies like *The Story of O*. I had no concept of that way of having sex and wanted to turn her on. So I said, "If I threw this ketchup bottle against the wall would that turn you on?" She went: "Yeah." So I did it. I did it to *heighten* the moment. It kind of worked for her. Me, I was banned from the restaurant for a year. But I've given them a lot of publicity. And I met my wife there.'

Patricia Arquette was nineteen. It was late in the evening and she was with a group of friends at Canter's. Cage wandered in and saw her: 'She walked past me and said she'd just eaten liver and onions. I fell in love with her then and there. I said: "Listen, you don't believe me but I want to marry you." And she said no. And I said, "Then, put me on a quest. Anything. Let me prove how much I mean this." And so she went back to her table and she wrote this list down on a napkin of things she wanted. And the things, I began to realize, were impossible to get.'

Arquette's list comprised an autograph of writer and recluse J. D. Salinger, a black orchid, a fibreglass statue from one of the Bob's Big Boy hamburger restaurants and a wedding dress from a Tibetan tribe.

Cage roared off in search of what he thought was the easiest target: the orchid. 'I had a Harley-Davidson FLH at the time – black, I had it all tricked out, it was beautiful, police special belt drive – and I said, "Can I have a black orchid, please?" And they said: "There's no such thing as a black orchid." I knew something was askew. So, I said, "Gimme the purple orchid." I took that and went to the art store and got some black paint and I went to her house and I rang the doorbell and she wouldn't answer the bell. I saw her peeking through the curtains on the top floor. I whipped the flower out of my leather jacket very cavalierly and spray-painted it black in this big show that only a twenty-three-year-old would do and I went up to the door and gave it to her and she went, "Thank you." She was terrified.'

He then went off in search of a Salinger signature. 'I found one at a place on Beverly Boulevard. It was a handwritten letter to a woman. It was a lot of money, $2,500. A lot of people don't believe it because they know that J. D. Salinger never signed anything. My manager Gerry Harrington is friends with J. D. Salinger's son, who says his father never signed anything. But this was a letter he wrote so I bought it, I had it.'

He put it in a cigar box with an apricot and a Dominican cigar and left it on Arquette's doorstep: 'She was playing hopscotch in the street with her girlfriends. Hopscotch! I was driving a Peugeot, a silver one, and I pulled up and left the cigar box and drove off. She was off the Richter scale . . .'

Arquette's version of events is close: 'It was a very romantic story. He had me fill out this quest like a princess. He kept coming after me and I thought it was a joke he was making on me with his friends or something. I didn't understand. I didn't think I was the kind of girl that this kind of guy would be falling all over so I didn't understand why he was pursuing me so hard. He asked me to fill out this list and I thought, "Well, it's kind of fun and I'll put all these things like Salinger's autograph and a black orchid and he'll go away. The next day I hear this motorcycle outside my mom's house and I peek out the window and there he is with a purple orchid and a black spray-paint can and he's spraying it!

'Every day a new thing would show up at the door and the deal was when he'd finished I had to marry him. I had never gone on a date with him! I said, "OK, OK, *stop!* I'll go on a date." We did. We were kissing and kissing and kissing. I got a burn on my face from his beard. Every time we'd go to a restaurant I'd end up running out of there. He never got to eat. He'd always be chasing me down the street. "Please, I'm hungry – don't run away so we can be friends."'

They went away together to Mexico. It was intense and Cage reveals: 'I remember being so in love that I wasn't able to have sex because I was paralysed. I couldn't perform on that level.'

Then, in Mexico City they tried to fly to Cuba where Carmine Coppola was conducting *Napoleon*. Cage intended to marry Arquette in Havana. But the bureaucracy of Mexico tripped him up. He had a temper tantrum – as almost everyone does – at the airport and they weren't allowed on the plane. My plan was to abduct her to Cuba and marry her while my family was there but I got derailed at the Mexican airport because they couldn't find my tickets and I had a tantrum. That scared Patricia. She didn't like how I was yelling at everybody.'

They stayed in Mexico, listened to bands and then returned to Los Angeles. Arquette also returned to her boyfriend, the musician Paul Rossi. But she stayed in touch with Cage: 'We'd talk on the phone and he'd say, "Marry me," and I'd say, "I have a boyfriend. Don't talk to me that way." I'd ring him and he'd say, "I have a girlfriend." Sometimes I'd call him and say, "Why don't you pick me up and take me to have my hair done?" And I wouldn't have seen him in six months . . .'

This most unorthodox romance went on for more than eight years. Cage could never forget her but Arquette's attention was distracted.

She found she was pregnant with Paul Rossi's son, which may have blocked her romance with Cage but was a spur to her career: 'I really didn't think I was too good at acting but when Enzo was born that didn't matter any more. Enzo made me successful, made me commit to something. I knew that I had to try. I had to be a breadwinner.'

While Arquette worked at being a single mother and a movie star, the lovestruck Cage was pursuing work – and women. And idiosyncrasy. Love had confused him: 'It's not two Cupids holding hands or sugar and spice and everything nice or puppy dog tails. But I can't define love. I think it does break your heart and ruin things. But I think it's a necessity.

'I like the mystery. I like having time to dream things and build on the passion before acting on it. I think the whole process of courtship is a good one where you don't just jump into the sack right away and have sex immediately.

'I think you can almost have sex by just looking into someone's eyes. I like being able to look into a woman's eyes and feel as if I could crawl off the edge of the universe. Love *is* a necessity.'

For him, work was also. There were few actors of his age with such a impressive résumé.

He was still splitting his time, with his Burmese cat Louis, between his castle and his two-bedroom apartment in an old building in Hancock Park. The neighbours weren't sure about his nocturnal habits: his day would begin around noon or one p.m. and run through the night till around five a.m.

Past residents and visitors may have been more approving. George Raft was said to have painted a caricature on the lift shaft and Bing Crosby supposedly kept a flat there for away-from-home hanky-panky. For several decades, Mae West lived across the street.

After *Moonstruck* he was after something different. He got it with *Vampire's Kiss*, a low budget black comedy in which he played a literary agent convinced that a sexy vampire played by Jennifer Beals has turned him into one of the undead. 'It was the movie nobody wanted me to do – particularly my agent and my lawyer. I make my own decisions but it was hard because everybody said don't do it. I said, "Yes," then pulled out. Then Judd Nelson and Dennis Quaid were in and they pulled out.

'Finally, I went back in because otherwise I'd feel like a coward. It was important for me to take a fucking chance. It was just a great screenplay. It grabbed me by the collar and screamed, "If you don't do this movie you're a fucking coward!" It wasn't a practical choice to make but it was an honest choice. I figure that in order to succeed in the film business you can't be afraid to roll the dice. And as long as I'm betting I want to bet everything I've got.

'I used to watch the German expressionist films when I was a boy and they were much more horrifying than anything today – claustrophobic and really spooky. I would have nightmares about them. With *Vampire's Kiss* I saw an opportunity to say, "Well, this man is insane and so I have a right to do what I want. I can use some of those old German facial expressions and hand gestures and combine it with sound." That's what I was so excited about. And that excitement resulted in the cockroach. The director wanted me to eat raw eggs but I felt it had been done before. Every muscle in my body was telling me not to eat the roach and I remember it biting the tip of my finger before I ate it. I was definitely in some altered state – thinking about Samurai warriors. It didn't just crunch. It was soft, kind of like chicken, and there was something sensual about it. I felt kind of sorry for it.

'I did it because I wanted the audiences to have a visceral experience. I think it also added a new level of danger to the character I was playing. I like people to wonder. I like disturbing people. I don't like to discuss my technique. It's kind of like *The Wizard of Oz*. If you pull the curtain off you just see a little man talking through a megaphone.'

But when the curtain was whisked away from *Vampire's Kiss* something magical was revealed: 'Everybody who participated in the film did it because they liked the material – it wasn't about money at all. It was the first film I did that I felt totally satisfied with after seeing. It wasn't an easy process making that film.'

Tell that to co-producer Barry Shils. 'Nic goes out on a limb and we needed that kind of boldness. There wasn't a lot of money involved but Nic didn't care. He has guts and he likes to gamble. At one point he wanted us to replace the mechanical bat we were using with a real one. He was worried that the toy one was flying too slowly and audiences would know it was a fake. We told him a real bat was out of the question. It was illegal. They carry rabies and he could be bitten. Nic said it didn't matter, he wanted it to look authentic. He tried to get us to get someone to go out into Central Park in New York and capture one.'

Cage lost the debate. But in one shower scene he decided to whistle and hum Stravinsky's *Petrouchka* and Shils complains: 'We had to pay for the rights to use Stravinsky. I asked him why he couldn't hum something in the public domain. Nicolas will go to great lengths to get the right effect.'

It worked on *Vampire's Kiss* which remains – even with *Leaving Las Vegas* – a 'pure' Nicolas Cage movie.

It was British director Robert Bierman's big screen début. He worked well with Joseph Minion's screenplay, allowing the film to hover on the brink of tastelessness and silliness. Cage is a Manhattan yuppie at his most obnoxious, a hot-shot literary agent who browbeats his secretary – the ravishing Maria Conchita Alonso – demanding that she concentrate on the pointless job of finding a ten-year-old missing contract.

At the same time Cage's character is puzzled why his relationships with women are so shallow. He regularly sees a cool psychiatrist – played by Elizabeth Ashley – but is an uncooperative patient. He's a perfect target for Jennifer Beals's vampire. Minion, who wrote Martin Scorsese's film *After Hours*, told a contemporary morality tale with humour, in which the vampire lifestyle becomes a useful metaphor for the rapaciousness of modern society.

The demand on Cage's talent was huge. He had to appear hatefully obnoxious yet pathetic in his progressive deterioration. Above all, he had *always* to seem funny. The film divided the critics but Terence Rafferty of the *New Yorker* wrote:

> Cage carries everything with a manic intensity that plays with throwaway ease but must have required the utmost energy and concentration – not to mention spontaneity.
>
> Alonso has a no less tricky assignment, as this most expressive of actresses succeeds in finding the humour in the mortification of the secretary. That this woman is a Latino who dares not quit her job makes it all the riskier to make her the object of such continual abuse. That the film makers get away with it is actually liberating; shrewdly, they've realized that if they proceeded timidly it would not have worked any more than soft-peddling Cage's callous treatment of a beautiful young black woman (well played by Kasi Lemmons) would have worked.
>
> *Vampire's Kiss* is not putting the bite on these women but on Cage's agent, whose absurd power-tripping nastiness characterizes so much of everyday life in the big city. It starts off with as strong a sense of eeriness and impending doom as any film since *Wolfen*. The opening credits appear over a montage of inhuman cityscapes, accompanied by disquieting music. After a few minutes, we hear an indistinct voice-over that turns out to be Cage telling his psychiatrist about a recent sexual encounter. "I wanted her to disappear," he says.
>
> After another liaison is interrupted by a bat zooming around his apartment, he admits to his shrink that he found the bat more

exciting than the girl; the next night he brings home yet one more pickup, sultry Rachel (Jennifer Beals). In the throes of passion, Rachel bites his neck and Peter realizes ... *dum dum dum* ... she's a vampire!

During the next week or two, he develops strange symptoms: an aversion to light, fear of crosses, blackouts, a hunger for roaches. Most of all, he terrorizes his secretary. For its first half hour, *Vampire's Kiss* seems to be a total catastrophe. Cage plays his character insanely over the top from nearly the first scene, affecting what sounds like a particularly irritating Philadelphia accent – is that a redundancy? – alternatively shrieking and mumbling in manic mood shifts. Horrific moments are staged for laughs. Everything seems out of control.

At a certain point, however, it becomes clear that the humour – and the lack of moderation – is wholly intentional. His attitude towards his secretary is reprehensible before his vampirism starts. When he chases her through the office and corners her in the ladies' room, his insane behaviour is seen as merely amusing by his colleagues and as a boss's prerogative by the underlings.

Cage delivers a remarkable portrayal of a completely obnoxious jerk. He's so offensive from the start that no one really notices his transformation, not even when he starts skulking around New York wearing cheap plastic fangs, his shoulders hunched in imitation of Max Schreck's *Nosferatu*.

The real comparison here is to Roman Polanski's great *The Tenant*. Make no mistake: Robert Bierman is no Polanski. Where Polanski keeps humour and horror carefully balanced through every scene, Bierman, for much of the film, alternates the two effects. But by the end, which is both sad and funny, he seems to have achieved a synthesis.

This is basically Cage's show all the way. For pure weirdness *Vampire's Kiss* is without rival. It's also about the most *interesting* film of the year.

America's most admired critic Pauline Kael wrote: 'Cage is airily amazing. He does some of the way-out stuff that you love actors in silent movies for doing and he makes it work with sound. This daring kid starts over the top and just keeps going.'

Despite such important reviews the film did poorly at the box office but, with hindsight, many believe this wrinkle in the Dracula legend is not only a gem in Cage's career but in movie-making. Cage won a Best Actor nomination from the Independent Features West organization for his work as the despicably smug agent Peter Loew.

It was a movie that Cage truly cared about and he remains protective of it. When *Vampire's Kiss* was released on video the picture on the box displayed Cage in plastic fangs and a cape. He wanted blood: 'I never once wore a cape in the movie. Big business marketed it as some schlock vampire movie, some supernatural piece of shit! For a while there I felt that I couldn't win. I poured my heart into this and they put me in that stupid cape. What do I gotta do? When the video came out it really hurt.'

But he was already a winner. His last three leading ladies had been Holly Hunter, Kathleen Turner and Cher. He was credited with a formidable screen presence. *Vampire's Kiss* was a hit with important critics. He was impossible to typecast but, in Hollywood terms, highly bankable. And that is very cool. He was just beginning to realize his stature: 'Sometimes I wake up and say, "Totally incredible!"'

Wandering around Los Angeles he is stared at by women. Men like him but he is the kind of man women gaze at openly with a lingering fascination, although he is no hunk. Rather, it's his hangdog eyes, a look of vulnerability, that seem to attract them. It's a sensitive yet uncompromising posture. And it's a brooding look that says, 'Baby, I can be very dangerous.'

Flipping a wave of long chestnut hair away from his eyes, Cage doesn't fight the impression. He likes it, particularly the part about his seeming dangerous. 'I can be,' he says. He has also been called a sex symbol, which elicits from him a very knowing chuckle: 'Actually, there's nothing wrong with being a symbol of sex. It might seem a little silly, but it's fun too. I think sex really gets a bad reputation. I think a lot of frigid people automatically give it a bad name because they don't know how to relax. They blame it on sex itself, which is completely wrong. Sex is a good thing, a really cool thing, a really natural, correct thing to do.'

He likes discussing sex. And actresses: 'Holly is the only actress I've worked with who has been full of surprises with her acting. It was like she had a Felix the Cat bag of tricks and just kept pulling things out. Cher relied mostly on instinct. And her instincts are good ones but I do think she needs a good director. Otherwise, she's in trouble.' And Kathleen Turner, his nemesis? 'She is like a technician. She knows exactly what she's going to do and she does it. Me? I just don't want to get bored.'

He keeps active. His friends, like Crispin Glover from *River's Edge* and *Back to the Future* and singer-songwriter Tom Waits, are used to his habits. In the late 1980s Cage was almost completely nocturnal: 'What do I do all night? I sit in my bathtub, with a special kind of sea soap, and smell this salty piece of rope from the Santa Monica pier and try to transport myself to the ocean. Epsom salts, baking soda, sea salt and David Bowie's *Low* – that's a good bath. Or I'll stroll into the living room and watch my jewel-encrusted tortoise walk along the carpet. I'll watch my sharks swim.' He had two sharks – a pig and a nurse. Once there was a third: 'A lemon shark. A three-footer. But a clock fell into the water when I was on location and it got electrocuted. My ideal living space would have a study, a circular room, with my desk in the middle, and surrounding me completely would be an aquarium filled with salt-water and huge sharks, octopuses, and creatures of the sea. In effect, I'd be surrounded by the ocean. When I was growing up I always wanted to be a whale doctor or a marine biologist.'

But for the time being his 'space' was the two bedrooms in Hancock Park full of diverse art, including a Chagall lithograph. Cage says he didn't buy it 'for the sake of investment', but because he likes 'the distraction good art provides.' He has a similar attitude to food and calls himself a 'simple chef', who has 'respect for all the different food groups'. Faddish? Never. One dining companion Chez Cage reported a meal of alligator sausages and beaver meat as the main course.

This was after the brief encounter with Patricia Arquette and it was clear his mind was still on love and romance as well as sex and seafood: 'I think I need a great woman to become the best man I can be. If it's true romance, I don't find it fun. The passion is exciting but it takes forever to get over the breaking up.'

He ponders on a quote and decides:

'Man has in his thoughts debased sex to a decadent function but I have tried to transcend that consciousness and I have fought to lift it into the realm of symbolic mystery.'

Impressive nonsense, of course.

'Yeah', laughs Cage, 'but I've never said that before. It felt good.'

Chapter Thirteen
Low Flying, Fast Driving

'Everything is weird on top and wild at heart.' Laura Dern, as Lula in *Wild at Heart*, 1990.

On America's big-ratings *Saturday Night Live* they called them *alternative* comedians. Cage was an alternative actor. He was tagged the odd man out among young stars, a spooky-ride king, a neo-expressionist screwballer, flaky *and* exhilarating. However, he was living mainstream and well – too well.

His castle in the Hollywood Hills was devouring money so he agreed to star in *Fire Birds*, which was Tom Cruise's *Top Gun* but with helicopters. 'I had bought the house and got in over my head and I realized I was in serious need of money. I'm not into the starving-artist syndrome. People who do their job well should be paid well. I kept saying I should do a little movie that would be good for my soul but I needed the money. I admit it. I was not being true to my instincts but I felt like I wanted to do a role which was this straight American character.

'I suppose I wish I hadn't done it but in the end it was worth it. I've always made myself spend too much money to force myself to work. I think I'm afraid of being too comfortable but what I buy are objects and they're to be respected and appreciated but they're not to be worshipped. But no matter how beautiful they are they are objects and work is what makes me happy.'

Not every time – he has made wrong moves but he never likes to admit them. Or apologize for them. However, his explanations always sound sincere. He always has his reasons.

It's like *Peggy Sue Got Married*. The critics either dismissed him in that movie or tore his performance to shreds. He says, with a lopsided grin: 'It was an important film to *me*. It was at that time I began to re-evaluate the kind of style I wanted to choose as an actor. That was when I began to realize that I could get a little more off kilter and try something less naturalistic and more abstract. That excited me. It sort of refurbished my whole interest in what I was doing.'

Cage *is* interesting. He is straightforward and clearly determined to establish his niche in films rather than in Hollywood. By the 1990s there was no grandstanding. He would turn up to talk driving his black Mercedes in black T-shirt, jacket, jeans, cowboy boots and a grin: 'I'm not going to shed my black clothes for ever. It's in my nature.'

In 1990 his agent was the powerful Ed Limato. For a lot of people *Raising Arizona* had been Cage's breakthrough movie but the more commercially minded, including Limato, believed it had been his role as Cher's off-beat love in *Moonstruck*.

'Ed was pushing for that but I was hesitant. Then, I was pushing for *Vampire's Kiss* and he was hesitant. I had a bad experience with the film. I really wanted to do it and I was thrilled with the movie that *I* saw. Then, the movie was released and somebody took a blowtorch to it and re-edited the whole thing. It was like losing an old painting. It was something that was very hard to deal with. People just didn't get it. A few people did and that's cool.

'I did it for no money. I just did it because I needed to do it. I needed to get it out of my system. I think it made me think about the business aspect of movies and that I should do something conventional so that I get the price up and get the clout so I could do another *Vampire's Kiss* and have control.

'That could backfire too because that's not pure. That's sort of a game plan and I guess for now I want to stay pure. I've heard that Nicholson does one movie in every four for commercial reasons. Michael Caine is kind of an inspiration because he can do anything from *Jaws IV* to *Mona Lisa* to *Blood and Wine* with Nicholson and maintain this integrity and get well paid for it. I don't know how he does it – he's always respected no matter what film he's in. He's an actor for hire and there is no pretence about it.

'The eighties for me were really a learning process. I started off when I was seventeen and I didn't know what I was doing. I still don't but in a way I like that. I've had to learn publicly about film and it's a trial and error thing. The nineties are more exciting for me because I feel a bit more in touch with what it is I want to do.

'*Fire Birds* was as unlikely for me as you could get but I was challenged by it and the people involved wanted to work with me. They made a deal that was respectable and made me feel good and got me out of some debts that I was severely into with the house. But this straightforward American hero was a challenge.'

Fire Birds (originally titled *Wings of the Apache*) was a project from British director David Green, who had gone to Hollywood following the success of *Buster*, in which Phil Collins and Julie Walters starred in the story of the Great Train Robber. He got together an intriguing cast: Cage, the taciturn Tommy Lee Jones and Sean Young. Co-starring with them were AH-64A helicopters – the US Army's $10-million-apiece attack choppers.

In the movie the high-tech whirlybirds were part of a task force sent to an unnamed South American country to battle drug barons. But pivotal to the action was the romance between Cage and Sean Young. It didn't work. Chemistry? There was none. The action overshadowed the characters – and that is what Cage plays best.

He had something else on his mind. Fatherhood. After his fling – and that's exactly what it was – with Patricia Arquette, the lovelorn Cage had turned into a dating machine. He says he was looking for a stable relationship, which is always hard to find but even harder if you are a high-profile 'wild' Hollywood star. But model Kristina Fulton snared him. He says they seemed perfectly compatible and they were living together. But there were problems: 'I don't like people to be hurt but living life as an actor it's hard not to hurt people. There is a distance in relationships. It's the business. You're away a lot. It's hard not to hurt or be hurt. It's just one of the brutal facts. I've only met actresses and models and there's been an instability there.'

On location on the outskirts of Tucson, Arizona, he had to deal with a complicated love life *and* Fulton's pregnancy. He asked anyone who would listen: 'What should I do? Should I marry her? What can

I do?' The couple decided not to marry but to stay together and raise Weston, who was born on 26 December 1990. Cage has grown into the paternal role but before his son was born he was nervous and turned to his work.

'Nic was the leading man we wanted,' said David Green. 'He had youth appeal as well as the look of an action man. He *fitted* his pilot's flying outfit. I think it was a new sort of show for him and he went for it. He was a total professional. Like me, he was looking for a very American movie. I thought, as a British film-maker, I could bring a fresh perspective to an American genre. Nic was in that position too.'

One challenge facing David Green was to keep his stars alive, because his movie included elaborate special effects and many flying sequences. 'The number of helicopters that have crashed on film sets is legendary. We had more 'copters in the air than have ever been used in a film. More than a hundred helicopters were used on the ground and as many as four were flying at one time and in close proximity.'

Safety briefings, including on-site walk-throughs with special-effects personnel, preceded all filming involving pyrotechnics, stunts or aerial work and were mandatory for all department heads, pilots, the aerial director, aerial co-ordinator, stunt co-ordinator and others. Helicopter safety procedures included communications between ground and air at all times. Only necessary designated personnel were permitted within a hundred feet of the aircraft.

The risk factor didn't bother Cage. He liked it: 'There is a kid inside me who likes helicopters and fireworks. Film is a big-business industry and that game needed to be played to ensure that I continued to work.' He and Tommy Lee Jones did their own stunts for the film's ground action sequences and their own flying – accompanied by a real-life Army pilot.

But it never felt right to Cage: 'They were trying to do a rehash of *Top Gun* and I couldn't fit that bill. I knew when the producers came into the trailer and said, "We want you to smile more," that I was miscast.'

Whether it was down to miscasting or his on-screen romance with Sean Young that went wrong or simply that helicopters were not his vehicle, the movie didn't fly at the box office – or with the critics. 'He never listens or sees anybody else in a scene, being too busy monitoring his own utterly mysterious attention-getting responses,' complained Vincent Canby in the *New York Times*: 'This ludicrous action-romance was marred by Cage's tendency to indulge in scenery-chewing episodes of overacting.'

Well, that would seem to suggest that it was time for Sailor Ripley. With such a character Cage couldn't really *under*act.

Wild at Heart was the watershed of Cage's career. It was the much-awaited film from David Lynch, the maestro of lyrical horror, following the fanfare over his *Blue Velvet* – which revived Dennis Hopper's career and introduced Laura Dern to the big time – and before the worldwide intrigue with *Twin Peaks* on television. Cage as Sailor, who calls himself an 'outlaw in love', was Elvis on the lam in a snakeskin jacket. Rarely have a role and an actor collided at just the right time and place.

Cage's favourite time is evening and the place is the La Brea tar pits in Los Angeles. The pits are ringed by a tall chain-link fence but through the mesh you can see a watery pool rippling with methane bubbles from the fissures below. Cage seems mesmerized by it: 'It's very prehistoric. It brings back memories. As a kid I used to come here and imagine that the bubbles were from sea monsters. The funny thing is there still are sea serpents. Imagine what it was like for Columbus to see a giant squid for the first time! That was a sea monster. The white shark, the blue whale . . . but we've discovered all our monsters.'

The roles that led up to Sailor Ripley had their primal aspects: Peter Loew in *Vampire's Kiss*, and the self-proclaimed 'Wolf' in *Moonstruck*, who courts Cher to Puccini. 'I wouldn't have been able to say that but now that it's mentioned I might have to agree. Though I have cats and I do watch *them*. And some of what they do stays in my mind and appears later. Especially when they have sex.'

Although he hit at the right time it always seems that Nicolas Cage was born out of synch. Hollywood could not – and still cannot – understand him. Although the studio system that controlled the stars of the past has long gone, an understanding exists that the players will allow themselves to be guided. The agents and packagers have taken over from the studio moguls and their sycophants but the rules are pretty much the same. Cage has never understood that. Cher found the point, explaining: 'When you strip everything away, he is still a Coppola.' And Coppolas don't like authority, or anything that they think will chain down *their* way of working.

David Lynch was perfect for Nicolas Cage, who says: 'David is like a criminal director. He's not concerned with Establishment laws and rules. He just does what he does and it's honest. He's constantly sculpting and fishing. A scene can turn into a comedy or into a heavy horror in a fraction of a second. He's very much a sculptor, a spontaneous sculptor.'

Lynch conjured up a road movie, a 'Wizard of Odd' packed with a cast of weird characters spinning around the romance of Sailor Ripley with radiant Laura Dern's Lula Pace Fortune. Cage – doing his Elvis – talked in a melodically guttural macho purr, and rock 'n' rolled in a lizard-lidded cool world of his own. The movie was – and stands as – a poetic parody, but also a homage: 'This *is* the sort of movie Elvis should have done.'

On their travels Lula and Sailor meet a coven of Lynchian figures, brought to life by Isabella Rossellini, Diane Ladd (Dern's mother), Willem Dafoe, Harry Dean Stanton, Crispin Glover and John Lurie.

With their uncensorious imaginations the collaboration of Lynch and Cage makes perfect sense – unlike their movie.

'There are a lot of things that make Nic unique,' says Lynch. 'His way of delivering lines, his look. He's got an ability to do really heavy things and goofy things. His attitude encouraged me to think of things for him to do, because he's so good at going into strange places. You give him an idea and he grabs onto it like crazy. He's like a wild dog on a leash.'

In turn, Cage says of his director mentor: 'David Lynch's movies are more real than Spielberg's – they're inside reality. I think dreams are gifts so I try to find a film that will do those things, whether it's a dream state or just being insane.'

Lynch – Mel Brooks fondly dubbed him 'Jimmy Stewart from Mars' – says that Cage was his first and only choice for Sailor. The pair had been casual acquaintances. They had met at local shops and at the Musso and Frank, the home of the best martini and 'steak and fries' in Hollywood: 'We both like to sit at the counter there. I like to stare at the chimney above the grill. It reminds me of old Hollywood, and Nic is a Hollywood type of guy. You know, a big smile, sunglasses, kind of the gold El Dorado type of thinking. He could be either a Las Vegas performer or a big movie star. He happens to be a big movie star.'

The same night on which Lynch introduced Cage and Dern, the historic Pan Pacific movie theatre burned to the ground only a few streets away. 'The film has a lot to do with fire, so that was kind of interesting. I sat opposite Nic and Laura and the whole time I'm sitting there, I'm thinking how both of them have this same quality of being beautiful and not beautiful, intelligent and yet so understanding of "ordinary". And Nic seems to know . . . to be older than he is.'

Cage agrees: 'I do feel older that my years but I don't know why that is. A lot of times on the set I thought David looked younger than I did [Lynch is fifty]. I think I wear darkness on my face more than he does. But I don't know if that's because I'm just fascinated by it or because it really is there. It's always been that way.

'Elementary school was tough because I was considered too serious. I think I was voted "most stubborn", which is really a boring award. Maybe I was trying to be a little like my father in those years. He was very serious. But I don't have that mannerism any more. I mean, I don't *want* to be taken seriously. Like sometimes, I'll wear a T-shirt that says ITALIA on it. I visited a friend of mine, and his wife said to me, "Nic, it's impossible to take you seriously with that stupid T-shirt on." Well, that was exactly the idea. It's funny, people who don't know me say I come off very old. My closest friends tell me I'm a kid.'

With Lynch it was playtime.

'When you talk about various levels in acting the same is true with David in *Wild at Heart*. It's a very universal film, operating on different levels. It operates on a comedic level, it operates on a real level. And also on an absurdist level. Like, there's this gritty road movie, this love story on the road emanating through a *Wizard of Oz* tonality which gives it more texture and colour.'

In other words this southern Gothic odyssey was a wild, over-the-top movie-making adventure. During the filming of a getaway scene involving Sailor and Lula outside a seedy hotel in New Orleans's French Quarter the director left the scripted plan as the couple prepared to escape in a 1965 Thunderbird convertible. As the onscreen lovers, for the thirteenth time, made the five-yard dash for the cameras they encountered unexpected turbulence: Lynch had grabbed a few dozen locals, many of them transients staying at the hotel, to give the duo a rousing farewell cheer. Then Lynch was ready for his next look at the underbelly of New Orleans. 'He likes things in a certain amount of decay,' said Julie Duvic, who scouted locations for *Wild at Heart*. 'His imagination is a little off.'

While filming a scene at a flea-infested bungalow in Los Angeles, Lynch displayed his penchant for witty surrealism. As Dern and Cage's characters look into the courtyard they see three fat actresses – naked apart from veils – making a porno movie. 'It added nothing to the plot directly. It was just something crazy David wanted to do,' admitted co-producer Monty Montgomery.

A film-maker for nearly two decades, Lynch has made weird part of his business card. He created the 1977 cult classic *Eraserhead* involving a spastic woman and a mutant baby. He conjured up a severed ear and arguably the cinema's greatest sadomasochistic madman in *Blue Velvet*. He turned John Hurt into John Merrick in the distinguished *The Elephant Man*.

'When people first meet David, they expect him to be neurotic and crazy and sick, but he's not,' says his former lover and star Isabella Rossellini. 'It's just that he looks at life in a different way. When David speaks, he sounds like he just got off the Greyhound bus from Iowa. But underneath that Jimmy Stewart look you find a darker side.'

It's that shadowy, subterranean world that Lynch explores in *Wild at Heart*. The movie follows twenty-year-old Lula and Sailor Ripley as they flee across America from Lula's vengeful mother and the hitmen she hires to subtract a few years from Sailor's life. 'It was my road picture except there wasn't a role for Bob Hope,' said Lynch.

Cage was thrilled with his walk on the wild side. 'I like things pushed to the edge of reality.' But reality intervened in New Orleans. A crew member told Lynch towards the end of filming that a blonde woman had arrived and said, 'Hey, y'all need a whore? I'm a real one.' When Lynch heard, he laughed, paused and then asked, 'Golly, can we still get her?'

In Cannes for the world première of the movie, Lynch decided to leave his shoelace untied 'for good luck'. In America he didn't need luck – millions of TV viewers had tuned into the final episode of *Twin Peaks* and ABC TV announced that they were bankrolling the show for another year – and it seemed that he didn't at the Film Festival because he was awarded the Palme d'Or for *Wild at Heart*. With Isabella Rossellini at his side he wore a quiet smile and said with no apparent irony: 'It's a true dream come true.'

When *Wild at Heart* was shown at Cannes the movie fraternity debated Lula's contention that the 'whole world's wild at heart and weird on top'. The film is about obsessive imagery and compulsive behaviour: half the characters walk on crutches, heads get crushed, punctured and flown sky high, a dog trots past with a severed hand in its mouth and just about everybody chain-smokes, sometimes two cigarettes at a time.

The critics at Cannes were bemused. Some attacked Lynch's 'graphic visions of violence', and in reply he said, 'I have even worse.' A line from the movie summed it all up. Sailor says to Lula: 'The way your head works is God's own private mystery.'

But the film was no mystery to Cage: 'I understood where David was going at all times. He has a freedom and I understand that need for freedom. That is what I'm always after. Acting has been my ticket to freedom so I can't ever bad-mouth acting. It gave me a way out both financially and psychologically. I'll tell you this. I think if I wasn't acting I would probably be dead because I would – I mean, it has been a tremendous outlet for anger and feelings. It's been an escape process. Without getting personal, all my life I have generated these intense feelings. It's my nature to use extreme terms. I'm always black or white. It's very hard for me to be grey.

'I would have probably turned to crime. I guess I should be careful what I say but I have at times felt criminal tendencies but because of the work I have been able to release it. I've kept it on film. I'm attracted to outlaw characters, some sort of sociopath who can get through the problem and the circumstances and rise above it and reach a place of dignity and morality. These are the kind of characters I dig. I don't identify with one particular character who has been on film but I've seen a lot of movies where I have felt part of myself in the same situation in a fantasy world.

'I think that Stanley Kubrick's *Clockwork Orange* inspired me and that character inspired me. I think that *East of Eden* inspired me. I saw that film when I was fifteen and I identified with this situation, this need for the love from the father, the wanting to be acknowledged. I think it was that film that really made me decide to become an actor. I watched it and it moved me in such a way that no piece of music or book could do.

'It's always the possibilities of what you can do with a role that attract and Sailor was certainly attractive. David's previous films suggested to me that he has a very personal vision of the world. Going in I was confident that I could be spontaneous and fresh and that he would find things that lend themselves to this exciting world that he's created.

'It's a road picture in a sense that the two lovers on the run is a perfect formula for meeting interesting characters. With David's imagination those characters on the road get pretty extraordinary. It's like love in hell. These people love each other and they stick together – and there are some dark forces on the road they encounter.

'And there's a little bit of evil – well, I don't know if it's evil – in Sailor Ripley. He's kind of like an old Corvette in a snakeskin jacket needing a tune-up. He breaks down every now and then. Sailor's saving grace is that the whole reason for his actions is his love for Lula. The movie starts at a point where a lot of films end. You begin with these two characters madly in love, there isn't a conquest to go through. They're already there and it's where you take it from there that's exciting.

'It starts violently and you wonder how you are going to sympathize or get in step with a character after he brutally killed somebody. But it isn't a murder, it's manslaughter. You begin to realize that his intention is always to make his love happy. I felt at home with David directing, and in lots of ways I wasn't trying so hard as I have in the past because I trusted him. A lot more natural flow.

'And Laura as an actress is very bold and free-spirited and she can play off anything. I don't think she is the kind of actress who could ever be stumped. Her reactive ability is pretty remarkable. If I want to go to Jupiter she'll match that and take it to Saturn. She's out there and can keep up with anything and throw some curve balls back. It makes for an exciting combination.'

But he says that it was not as exciting off-screen as rumour broadcast. There have been many reports of an extremely close friendship between the film's two stars. Cage throws out the old chestnut, quite seriously: 'For the record we're good friends and that's it. Lovers we're not. We're dealing with a movie here that is extremely sexual and you can imagine the stories *that* generates. As far as my love life goes – I don't know what it is about that phrase that bothers me but it reminds me of a toothpaste commercial – I've always fuelled from a relationship. When I say fuelled, I mean it's motivated me and inspired me. My relationships have always been tumultuous, kind of unstable. Love is a very interesting emotion. It can make you crazy, it can make you happy, it can make you jealous, it can make you want to kill someone, it can make you want to cook for somebody. It inspires all sorts of feelings. I've been drawn to romantic films, which allow me to be free with the things that I do and also to purge some of the things that I feel. Love in general inspires me.'

Chapter Fourteen
Sunshine Superstar

'With Nic you never know what's going to happen. I've gone to the airport to drop him off and gotten on the 'plane.' Phil Roy.

I t was early evening when US Air flight 407 with 300 passengers and crew on board was about to begin landing procedures into San Francisco. The commuter flight from Los Angeles had been uneventful. Until the captain announced he was feeling unwell – and was losing control of the plane.

There were some screams and nervous shuffling of feet. And shock on Nicolas Cage's face. He had been playing captain and his joke backfired badly. 'I was bored and I wanted to liven up the flight. I had had a few drinks and wanted a bit of fun. So I got hold of the public announcement system and pretended I was the pilot. I announced I was not feeling too good and that I was losing control. I said we were losing altitude but to please bear with me. I meant it as a joke but everyone started freaking out and screaming. It was a bad experience. I got carried away. I didn't think the PA system was connected to the entire airplane. When members of the crew escorted me back to my seat and everyone found out what I had done they were furious. The crew told me I would be arrested when I got off the plane and, sure enough, there were three policemen waiting for me at San Francisco airport. They told me it was serious and I could go to prison. I explained that I was just having a bit of fun and told them I was very, very sorry. Fortunately, after a lot of talking, they let me off with a very stern warning. I was very lucky not to end up in jail.'

The incident took place on 20 July 1990 and San Francisco airport police sergeant James O'Donnell said: 'The pilot said Cage had been drinking and creating a disturbance in the first-class compartment.

He had gone on the PA system pretending to be the pilot and saying he didn't know how to fly the plane.

'We detained him when the plane landed and questioned him. The airline decided not to press criminal charges but the Federal Aviation Administration could have brought civil charges against him. If someone had been injured in the panic then it could have been a different story and Cage would definitely have been prosecuted. You can go away for a long time for something like that.'

Cage grounded himself after the incident but his career was still flying high. At least in the amount of work he had. *Wild at Heart* had made an incredible impact and he now had a cult following. People loved his Elvis.

He agreed to co-star in a graphically sexual movie. *Zandalee* was a strange picture and the central role was taken by British newcomer Erika Anderson. A stunning blonde, she was the extra-special sex interest. Cage was a 'wild at heart' artist who begins an affair with Anderson, the wife of his best friend played by Judge Reinhold.

Cage had great hopes for the film but it didn't work out. 'I was a sort of vampire of innocence. He wants to corrupt innocence because it's very seductive to him. He's almost like a messenger of temptation. It was a very different role than I played before and it was exciting for me to play a character who was not out there, not evil but amoral.'

Sex and violence. His grandmother, Divi, felt she couldn't enjoy his work. 'Make something we can all see. Why don't you make something me and my friends can go see and laugh?' she asked him. The timing was strange. Before his talk with Divi he had been watching an old television interview with Jim Morrison, who had clearly been drugged out of his mind. 'Morrison was saying, "I don't think we've done a song yet that conveys pure happiness." I thought to myself, "I should do that – something that's not so angst-ridden." Then Divi nagged me.

'I had reached a point where people had an idea about who I was. There is a narrow-minded consciousness in Hollywood. As shocking as it seems they really think you are the character you play. I did weird movies like *Wild at Heart* in which I had the snakeskin jacket and part of the time the prosthetic, the big, black-and-blue nose. I had done other weird movies so it was: "Nic Cage? He's the guy with the snakeskin jacket and wooden hand and he eats cockroaches. He's not right for that role, you know." You can intense yourself right out of the business. I've seen it happen.

'I neglected doing comedies for some time. Part of it was that I didn't want to acknowledge that side of myself. I knew it was there, though – I knew that in elementary school for it helped me to make friends and survive. I thought, Is it pretentious to be always brooding, always an upset and angry guy? I knew I could be funny but I didn't want to be funny. I wanted to be James Dean. But that was a turning point. I decided to tap into comedy . . .'

So began what Cage calls his 'sunshine trilogy' and the groundwork for what resulted in his Oscar: *Honeymoon in Vegas*, *Guarding Tess* and *It Could Happen To You*. Out went his speciality outsider oddballs and in came regular folk. Like 'The Flying Elvises'. Well, with Nicolas Cage there's got to be some shades in the sunshine. *Honeymoon in Vegas* had much going for it including his co-stars Sarah Jessica Parker and James Caan – Sonny in Uncle Francis's *Godfather* – and director Andrew Bergman. The plot was similar to that of *Indecent Proposal*. In that movie Robert Redford offers Woody Harelson a million dollars to spend the night with his wife, Demi Moore. Cage's film had more light, more sunshine.

Cage plays private detective Jack Singer who promises his dying mother, played by Anne Bancroft, that he will never marry. The Grand Prix attractions of Sarah Jessica Parker's Betsy make that difficult. He wants her and she wants a wedding or she's leaving him. They slip off to Las Vegas to marry but Cage loses his wife-to-be in a poker game with James Caan. A madcap chase to retrieve her follows before the arrangement becomes more than platonic.

By the late 1990s, Parker was one of Hollywood's busiest actresses (*Mars Attacks!*, *The First Wives Club*, *Extreme Measures*) but *Honeymoon in Vegas* was her first leading-lady role: 'It was my big chance and Nic knew it and helped. He was very generous – he was a lovely guy. He really wanted everyone to have a good time as well as work hard. I was very intimidated at the prospect of working with him because I had made all these assumptions about him based on his work. I thought he was going to be very odd and inaccessible but I found that he was really warm and funny and easy to work with. But Nic's choices were so funny that one take was basically wasted because I'd be laughing at what he was doing. You don't understand where he comes from because when you meet him he's a fairly normal person. He was playing normal in extraordinary circumstances as opposed to extraordinary in ordinary circumstances.

'Nic is very secure in his sexuality and manliness. I don't think he thinks he has to prove anything as a man. He doesn't use that bravado some people use. That's appealing and it's not calculated on his part.

'But something happens in the work environment for him, I guess, that is a catalyst for letting us into the deep recess of his peculiarity. After they yell "Action" – that's when you get the raving lunatic.'

Moving away from his off-centre, exaggerated characters was difficult for Cage. He may have wanted to make the sun shine for Divi and himself but he was a *dark* actor. 'My agent even said *Honeymoon in Vegas* was a long shot. Rick Moranis would have fitted better. There wasn't a whole lot in my work that would suggest I could play this everyday, ordinary guy.'

Director Andrew Bergman asked for a screen test. Cage did one happily. 'Nic wasn't exactly what I had pictured for it but he had a passion about it. He came in and he read and he *was* this guy,' said Bergman. 'I was surprised when he first presented himself for the role because it seemed odd. He had done such odd things. But he read and he was sensational.'

So was the movie, especially the memorable scene in which Cage finds himself on plane full of skydiving Elvis impersonators. After *Wild at Heart* and a *Saturday Night Live* appearance as Elvis, it seemed Cage was becoming obsessed with the King: 'For a while the Elvis thing was just happening and it led from one thing to another. I have a real problem with Priscilla Presley. I thought her book *Elvis and Me* was pretty much a big insult and it made him look like a villain. Whether or not he was, I don't know. I could never do that to someone I was in love with – trash them nationally.

'I like what Elvis turned into physically. I know that he probably wasn't feeling well but he became really, really big. I like the suits that he wore and his operatic voice. He got pretty close to America's concept of a godlike image. The sideburns, the mutton chops. I think it's pretty impressive and slightly ridiculous and I like things that are slightly ridiculous. That gives them a universal quality, the absurd. I like Elvis's later years.

'One night I was watching the documentary *This Is Elvis* and by the time we got to him doing karate in a jumpsuit I was just howling on the floor at the tragedy and absurdity of the situation. And that's when I knew I loved Elvis. I mean, he was the hot rebel in the fifties, an icon, and he was King Lear and the buffoon by the end. I felt his career was the ultimate myth.'

He says it is also a myth that playing 'ordinary' can curtail an actor: 'You can be extreme because what's happening is so frustrating and alarming. That kind of jealous, paranoid frustration is a gas to play.'

With Bergman, who also wrote *Honeymoon in Vegas*, he found a partner in his work. The director says: 'I have a tendency to italicize words in the script and there were times when Nic would just take the italicized words and just knock them over the fence in ways I never expected. Then he'd say, "Was that too over the top?" And I said, "If it's over the top I'll let you know. There's a lot of room at the top here." And there was.'

And not just on film. Sarah Jessica Parker says Cage freaked her out by 'making these insane bets on roulette'. Filming was on location in Las Vegas. The casinos were open all day every day. A temptation indeed for Cage: 'When you're living in Las Vegas for a couple of months it's impossible to walk by the tables and not throw something down to see what happens. The whole casino is geared so you do that. You can't find where you want to go, you can't find exits easily, the rooms are pumped with oxygen so you can't sleep. You're always up and you go downstairs and you gamble. I was making small bets – fifty dollars on red or black – but wasn't getting off on them so I started going for the bigger numbers. It made Sarah Jessica a little nervous. But I wasn't the guy at the baccarat table betting a million dollars. At one point I was betting ten grand. She was getting ill. I lost ten grand and couldn't get it back. I went up to my room and ran on the treadmill for about an hour so I could feel better about myself.

Then I set my alarm for about half an hour before the film set call. I went down to the table and bet twenty grand and got all my money back. Then I stopped. I never bet again. I didn't like the way it made me feel. The only feeling that's more poignant than being a winner is the feeling of being a loser. I don't like that feeling so I never did it again. If I had lost the twenty thousand dollars I would have gone to forty, eighty, a hundred and sixty until I got it back. I was going to get my money back.'

Financially, *Honeymoon in Vegas* was an all-round success. It also gave Cage mass appeal, even if the film was the antithesis of his ambitions. And that was part of the reason he was taken by *Red Rock West*, a comic cowboy *noir* that co-starred Dennis Hopper and David-Lynch-favourite Lara Flynn Boyle. Director John Dahl was desperate for Cage to play the too-honest-to-lie drifter: 'He's a one-of-a-kind actor. One reason people cherish him is that he plays very dark characters but never loses sight of that person's humanity. Look at *Raising Arizona* – he's absolutely charming but he's stealing babies and he's a hold-up man. It takes a special sort of actor to pull off the work that he does.'

Red Rock West was released on video in America before making it to cinemas. It has become a cult movie. And, to a degree, so has *Amos and Andrew*, a clever farce with racial overtones. Cage played small-time thief Amos Odell who becomes friends with Samuel L. Jackson's rich, successful black playwright Andrew Sterling. Sterling's white neighbours mistake him for a burglar when they see him in his home setting up his new stereo equipment. The comedy starts from there.

Cage struck up a strong friendship with Sam Jackson, who went on to establish himself as one of the greatest black actors of the 1990s with movies like *Pulp Fiction, A Time To Kill*, the action mainstream of *Die Hard 3* and 1997's *The Long Kiss Goodnight* with Geena Davis.

But Cage, despite his success, was having problems with the Coppola side of his family. He was not happy about missing out on *Godfather III* but he found solace, and work, with his brother Christopher who directed him in *Deadfall* in 1993. Cage played a 1950s-obsessed hitman – a comical cross between John Candy and Roy Orbison said one critic – in the film which lived up to its title at the box office. Cage recalls the movie this way: 'Bad wife. Really bad wig. Like a two-dollar wig that you get on Hollywood Boulevard. It was a chance to work with Christopher and he let me go for it in the regard that I could have fun with the make-up and disguise myself so I could really take advantage of the opportunity.'

However, director Hugh Wilson brought Cage more sunshine with *Guarding Tess*, in which he played a secret agent assigned to protect cantankerous former First Lady Shirley MacLaine. Cage was in heaven. The veteran MacLaine had a host of stories *and* lives. Cage played the reserved, straight-arrow minder to MacLaine's difficult woman-of-a-certain-age used to getting things her own way and the on-screen action mirrored their off-screen relationship. Given a different time and place, Cage and Maclaine could have been an 'item'. 'Maybe we were in another life,' offered the actress.

Forty years ago when Alfred Hitchcock was casting *The Trouble With Harry* he viewed the screen test of a nineteen-year-old Broadway actress called Shirley MacLaine, who did a brief song-and-dance act with a borrowed scarf as a prop. The rotund genius rumbled at her: 'My dear, you have the guts of a bank robber.'

And she still retains that devilish streak Hitchcock noticed all those years ago. She says: 'There is something in me even now that would push a peanut all the way down a street just to see if I could do it.' That 'something', of course, is the determination that creates career longevity.

And already Nicolas Cage had been in nearly twenty films. In the next one he would be Jimmy Stewart.

Chapter Fifteen
The Eclipse

'More Jimmy.'

Andrew Bergman directing Cage in *It Could Happen To You*.

ndrew Bergman and Cage had so enjoyed their *Honeymoon in Vegas* – as did the moneymen – that they planned to work together again. *It Could Happen To You* gave them the opportunity. The movie – variously titled *Cop Gives Waitress $2 Million Tip* and *Cop Tips Waitress* – was based on a true story. In the romantic comedy-fable, Cage is New York cop Charlie Lang who lives in Queens and walks the beat in Manhattan. Short of money for a tip at his neighbourhood coffee shop, he promises Bridget Fonda's waitress half his lottery ticket. Naturally, he wins. The jackpot amounts to $4 million and he hands over $2 million saying: 'A promise is a promise.' He says that three times as he ponders his next move.

The 'promise is a promise' refrain could have been written for James Stewart and that's how Cage played it: 'I was nervous that people were going to slam me for that because everyone knows that imitation is the worst thing you can do in acting. But I'm not sure that's true. I've always felt we all have a little bit of good and bad in us and that's what makes us complicated. But Charlie was good, good, good. I wanted to play him a little larger than life. Naturalism is a style that can be really effective but it can be really boring.'

Andrew Bergman believes Cage can never be boring: 'He makes ordinary guys interesting. There's nothing white bread about anything he does. There's something so unadorned about the way he says, "A promise is a promise," in that movie, it just gives you goose bumps.'

During filming Cage says Berman would urge: 'More Jimmy, more Jimmy.' And he admits: 'It was the Jimmy Stewart movie but I'm such a huge admirer – he's such an American icon – that I'd hesitate to say I was impersonating him. It was really more of a tip of the hat, a kind of homage. I do think he had what seemed to be a pure American innocence which trembled on the screen in a way which gave people hope. And there isn't a lot of that in the movies today. I'd done so many subversive, twisted characters on the darker side of things that it had been time to lighten up.'

Cage's next choice was unfortunate: he leapt into *It Happened in Paradise*. But it didn't 'happen'. The title was changed to *Trapped in Paradise*, which better reflected his feelings. The story of three brothers (Cage, Dana Carvey and Jon Lovitz) who rob a small town bank on Christmas Eve was filmed in Canada. Filming went on during the nation's coldest winter ever. 'I was very frustrated throughout the snow and the shoot,' said Cage. The movie was branded by one critic as 'the worst film ever made'. Perhaps it wasn't quite that bad but it made Cage yearn for the darker side of movie-making.

Little Junior Brown brought him back to it. He was a nightmare in a Charles Manson beard, a menacing movie monster and a character that will be remembered when Cage's sunshine boys are forgotten. *Kiss of Death* was a remake of a 1947 British film, which had starred Victor Mature, and Richard Widmark in his landmark role as a giggling psychotic killer who pushes an invalid in a wheelchair down a staircase. The 1994 version had Cage as crazy Little Junior but the fuss started when David Caruso was cast in the updated Victor Mature part. The lean, red-headed actor had established himself as a television superstar in *NYPD Blue* and had been accused of betrayal when he left the successful series to pursue a big-screen acting career. This was his first vehicle.

Cage recalls: 'My agent said, "You can't support David Caruso in a movie," but I really wanted to play the part.' He was also keen to work with director Barbet *Kiss of the Spider Woman* Schroeder. 'And I had to get back to wearing my black clothes. I thought, Why not? David's a good actor and I can support him. To me it was like I was finally going to be able to get the stink off me of the experience of *Trapped in Paradise.* And to blow out the state of schmaltz that I couldn't stand. I needed a change. I needed to get out of the sun. I was playing such do-good guys that I had to mix things up just to keep things interesting for myself. I needed to get back to the other kind of work that I like to do.'

In preparation for the role Cage spent two hours every day for eight weeks pumping iron and consumed eight meals a day, washed down with protein drinks, in a body building regimen. On-screen he was packed with menacing muscle. 'It's very moving to see that kind of dedication. That showed he was getting deep into the character,' said Barbet Schroeder who also pointed out: 'It's not very pleasant to go in that part of the human psyche.'

By then Cage had separated from Kristina Fulton, with whom he shares custody of their son Weston, and was living with model Kristen Zang. They had what he calls a 'tumultuous' relationship – and young Weston was suffering from asthma. In yet another of these weird coincidences in Cage's life, the character of Junior Brown was written as an asthma sufferer and he says he took inspiration from observing his son. But playing that role took its toll on Cage. The violence was constant and he worried as he played 'a guy who kills people with his bare hands'. To his surprise he found the role profoundly upsetting: 'I had just been trying to get the purity of the character – it was much simpler than it used to be. I was trying to be more truthful, not thinking so much, Oh, this will be shocking. But I realized on *Kiss of Death* that by the end of the day I was nauseous with it – threatening one guy with a cigarette or punching somebody to death. I just thought, I don't want to go there any more. I didn't want to go to that shitty little corner of my mind where I could actually see myself contemplating this behaviour.'

Cage was torn then – and he finds it a continuing dilemma – between being an actor and a parent. He would say, 'I'd rather be playing fire truck with my son,' but admitted later that he was also on the look-out for *the* role. But he acknowledges the 'extreme elation and worry that comes with fatherhood'. He says of its ongoing effect on him: 'I've slowed down. I'm a worrywart now. It brings a new kind of emotion, a depth that wasn't there before. I'm always aware that what I do could affect my son. You don't want to wake up hung over when you have a child. Being a father has had more of an impact on my life than anything else before or since. One of the amazing things about children is that they automatically cut out any debauchery or decadence left over from your youth. As soon as Weston was born I stopped smoking cigarettes and started buckling my seat belt. My lifestyle became dramatically different just by nature of becoming a parent.'

Because of the custody arrangements for Weston neither he nor Kristina Fulton may speak publicly about their situation. He is also reluctant to discuss the time he spent with Kristen Zang: he is not a kiss 'n' tell man. He was preparing to make *Leaving Las Vegas* when the clifftop relationship with Zang went over the edge: 'The split-up was a difficult one. It had been a stormy relationship. But it was also a sweet relationship. We just weren't right for each other. I was a lot older than she was. I had to get up early and she liked to sleep like you do when you're eighteen. She wanted to go to nightclubs. So there was a sadness when we had to split up and that sadness went into *Leaving Las Vegas* because the break-up came around the same time. A lot of the times I was saying, "I love you," I was just heartbroken.'

With Zang out of his life he went to seed. He let Little Junior Brown's muscle turn to fat and achieved the bloated alcoholic look of someone on a graveside helter-skelter. He had received the script for *Leaving Las Vegas* while filming *Trapped in Paradise* and he agreed to work for $240,000 instead of his usual $4-million-range fee. He went to work as though he was being paid $50 million.

He hit gold. *Leaving Las Vegas* delivered Cage an Oscar but also, for him, an endorsement of everything he was about. That mad, crazy bastard had a purpose, after all.

And a lot else was going on.

Patricia Arquette asked him to marry her. He got to co-star with his hero Sean Connery. And there was an offer to do another imitation – not of Jimmy Stewart this time, but of Jack Nicholson.

Crazy Cage as Jack the Lad. It had its in-built publicity machine.

Nicholson, indispensable Hollywood superstar, hell-raiser and womanizer: it's quite a story. Today he is balding, prone to an overlapping stomach and was sixty in April 1997. He says that doesn't bother him: 'The only thing wrong with turning sixty is there's no guarantee you'll be alive until you're a hundred and sixty.

'You know what I'm saying?'

Nicolas Cage understood.

Chapter Sixteen

Dancing with Ghosts

'We're from the same tribe.'

Nicolas Cage explaining his marriage to Patricia Arquette.

No Hollywood company had wanted to make *Leaving Las Vegas*: it was too depressing, 'a downer'. Eventually British director Mike Figgis raised the financing from a French company, Lumière – a comparatively paltry $3.5 million, which meant filming on the Las Vegas Strip without permits, using cheap super-16mm film stock, and depending on the dedication and good faith of his stars, Nicolas Cage and Elisabeth Shue.

Cage rented suites for two weeks at the Chateau Marmont on Hollywood's Sunset Strip so that he and Shue, then a graduate of light movies like two of the *Back to the Future* films and *Adventures in Babysitting*, could rehearse. Shue, who appeared in 1997 big-budget *The Saint* with Val Kilmer, also won an Oscar nomination for *Leaving Las Vegas* but lost to Susan Sarandon for *Dead Man Walking*.

'I thought she [Shue] was really witty and funny in her movies but I would not have been able to visualize her as Sera,' says Cage. 'When we were rehearsing at the Chateau Marmont I saw how devoted she was to the part. There is a tremendous amount of pain inside Elisabeth Shue. I don't know where it comes from but it's there and she's figured out a way to tap into it.'

Cage marvels at the edginess of the love story between Shue's sad-eyed Vegas hooker, Sera, and his Ben Sanderson, a failed Hollywood screenwriter drinking himself to death: 'It seemed the answer to all my prayers. I was fed up with the movies I was making and it gave me an opportunity to go back to a darker corner of my mind. I wanted to get out of the sun. The script astounded me. I was crying when I finished reading it. It is more than anything a story of unconditional love. It was definitely one of the coolest relationships I'd ever read in a screenplay. There's something about true love that is incredibly elusive. But Ben Sanderson found true love. Ben dies, but is it a sad ending? I don't know.'

The movie is a 112-minute suicide note as Ben pickles himself to death in every shade of alcohol from clear vodka to hazy tequila to the dark Jim Beam and Jack Daniels. Where Figgis and his players had a problem was getting audiences to accept a character who didn't want to help himself and who ignores not just a chance at life but at love. Like Cage's beloved Samurai warriors, his character Ben was also involved in ritual death. Of course, with Cage there is a certain beat to it all – he listened to Miles Davis throughout the twenty-eight days of filming – and in the opening shot he's seen trotting happily through a booze supermarket, loading up his trolley with bottle after bottle.

Figgis said: 'Nic is a dancer, a natural. That scene was meant to be seen much later in the picture but we put it in as the opening shot because in one image it establishes that this man is charming, he's pretty energetic and he's an alcoholic. The most impressive thing about Nic is the extent and depth of his preparation. One night he rang me and asked why I had specified that Ben drove a Jaguar. He argued that Ben would drive a black BMW like every agent in town. I agreed. He went through all the detail, through the clothes, the words, *everything.*

'He's something of an outsider in his family and I don't think he's ever completely gotten over some of the hurts. But for an artist that pain and insecurity is worth its weight in gold. It gives Nic acute powers of observation.'

There were was much to see in *Leaving Las Vegas.* When author John O'Brien shot himself through the temple in 1994, he left behind his Smith & Wesson pistol, a pizza box, an open bottle of vodka, his Macintosh computer and the novel *Leaving Las Vegas,* which Figgis had optioned as a movie just two weeks earlier. He was thirty-three. O'Brien had grown up in a working class suburb of Lakeside in Cleveland, Ohio, drinking Coca-Cola and listening to Bob Dylan in high school. He married Lisa Kirkwood and somewhere between Cleveland and Los Angeles he started drinking. In 1990, after a confetti of rejection slips, *Leaving Las Vegas* was published by Watermark Press, a small Kansas company.

Even as he was writing his next novel, *The Assault on Tony's*, which was found in his computer and published posthumously in 1997, he was drinking himself out of a job at a Hollywood coffee shop and his marriage.

On 10 April 1994, O'Brien's father Bill got a call from the Brotman Medical Centre in Los Angeles: 'John was beat up pretty bad. The doctors said he was going to die unless he stopped drinking. John didn't want to hear it: "No one is going to tell me I'm going to stop drinking."' That line is spoken almost verbatim in the movie by Cage. Three weeks later, Bill O'Brien heard that his son was dead.

Cage was acutely aware of what he was into with the film: 'I really felt the weight of playing a dead man's suicide note. This is a man who jettisons himself from his problems by hitting such an all-time low he no longer even feels pain.

'Ben is self-destructive. The hard thing to do was manifest the physical deterioration of an alcoholic to that acute a point. I guess John O'Brien had a very sad life. One day his family all came to the set and it was a kind of spooky day. I was wearing the exact same watch that John actually wore, which I had no idea of – coincidences like that seemed to seep through the veil or what was real and what wasn't. It was a very emotional thing. They were crying.

'A lot of tragedies are looked down upon now because of the lack of commerciality. But, as Mike Figgis says, it's an essential part of our culture because it prepares us for those rites of passage.

'Maybe by some definition my cousin's death [Francis Ford Coppola's son Gian-Carlo was killed in a boating accident while out with Griffin O'Neal in 1986] impacted my decision to do the movie although it's an entirely different situation. It got me thinking about death at an early age.

'At the time of the movie I was going through my own private wringer with the end of the relationship with Kristen. In a lot of ways that fuelled the performance. She and I were not happy at that point and it just went right into the character.'

When the film was over the romance was too. Cage read about the ravaging effects of alcohol ('It rips the lining off your stomach') and studied how alcoholics who are drying out deal with their drink-induced demons. He considers O'Brien's book more powerful than his film, explaining: 'My experience with the book was infinitely more because I wasn't seeing myself in it. When I watched the movie it was hard to subtract myself from it. I had been emotionally invested in the novel in a way that I had not been with a book since *A Clockwork Orange* and *Brave New World*.

'I remember Francis saying that novels are beautiful but that they're like old trains and that movies were the art form of our time. I think that writing is the root and that a great novel still tells the story in a way that movies are unable to tell it. There's the imagination and the pleasure of lying in bed, reading a chapter and visualizing it any way you want, hearing the voices any way you want to hear them and not having them blasted into your brain or your eyes.'

Before filming began Cage went to Ireland on a Guinness odyssey for two weeks 'to pick up some essence, some soul of the land of great writers and drinkers'.

Phil Roy, Cage's songwriting friend, went with him and reported: 'Basically we did Ireland by night. Nic hired a car and a driver with a monocle and we went from castle to country house. We picked up a girl at one castle – an aristocratic girl – and she stayed with us for three days. When Nic heard about a haunted house near Galway he said: "We got to go, man. We got to go." We went to Leap Castle, the ancestral home of the O'Carrolls, where this smelly apparition was meant to reside. We got a leg of lamb and went to the ruins. We lighted two candles and stayed all night waiting for the thing to appear. It didn't. At dawn we drove back to Dublin – a night out with Nic.'

When he arrived at the Gold River Resort in Laughlin, Nevada, to begin filming the staff expected movie-star antics. Instead, Cage booked in as Ben Sanderson and as soon as he got to his room he phoned room service for vodka and cranberry juice. 'He was really bizarre,' said Casino manager Brad Overfield. 'A lot of people thought he had to be drunk or on drugs because he was intense.'

Cage, who has never touched drugs, is a 500°-proof Method actor and Overfield's reaction was irritatingly familiar to him. He concentrated hard on *Leaving Las Vegas* and his work reflected the phrase Ben employed whenever any concerned person enquired after his health: 'Outstanding, sir!'

'Ben was happy. A man who has made the decision to die is not really fighting any more. Ben had let go. It's like, "We're going down the river and you can try to hold on but if you just let go you're riding, you're floating, you're up, you're smiling."

'And that seemed to be the way to do it and not have the lines become maudlin. I wanted Ben to be a kind of study in crumbled elegance – at one time probably the life of the party. A real social star with a great way with words, real command of the language, and a sense of style – the watch he wears, the way he dresses. And he's gone to a point where it's all starting to decay.'

Ben has burned his passport and family photographs, puts out his possessions for the garbage men and drives off into the Nevada sunset. He moves in with Sera on the condition that she doesn't try to stop him drinking. 'I got the feeling "Ben" meant "has been" and "Sera" in Spanish meant "to be",' says Cage. 'I don't believe in suicide but Ben found his destiny and he stuck to it. He sold his car, paid off the American Express bills and took his life into his own hands. In some eastern cultures that would be considered heroic. My opinion is that Ben is a victim of a bad family situation and maybe a divorce where he couldn't see his kid. I think men can respond to that. Our society in California isn't really geared toward the single father. It is very difficult for a man to have rights. It all goes to the mother and I'm sure that was something Ben was dealing with too.

'In the death scene I really wanted Ben to die saying, "Wow!" When you see death in films it's always portrayed as being painful and lonely. But we don't know. It could be anything – it could be a roller-coaster ride. I wanted it to be the beginning of a *trip*. Ben's in pain but he's seeing something. I felt the movie wasn't really about alcoholism. It was a love story about these two people.'

It was Cage's idea that, during his first encounter with Sera the prostitute and their failed attempt at oral sex, he would sing a song. 'I go to change in the bathroom for that scene,' recalled Shue. 'And he was out there singing this Batmobile song that he'd made up. It was just so odd. I kept laughing and he really got my attention. He drew me in and kept me looking honest.'

Cage and Phil Roy had written the song, titled 'Ridiculous', some years earlier:

'Blasting down the highway in the Batmobile,
You squealed with delight: We're going to Paris!
Caught between my passport and a root-beer float,
I turned the car around because you made fun of me.
You tell me I'm ridiculous . . .'

For Figgis it was an important moment: 'The singing conceit says Ben has enough innate grace and humility that sex is not his whole agenda. And consequently it made it a great sex scene.'

Shue understood too: 'When you're an actress you are very aware of the men you hope to work with because usually your parts are going to be supportive of those men and so you become extremely picky. You can't believe how many lines in the movie are Nic's – from "I'm a prickly pear" to the "kling-klang king". Nic's incredible range and freedom had inspired me over the years, and as out there as he is he's also out there in terms of his emotions and depth of feeling. The humour he brought to Ben was so devastating because it came from pain. And the tenderness. I love it that there are moments in film history where there is one person who can play a part and one person only.'

It is important to understand why Cage was that person: he inhabits his characters before as well as during filming. 'Nic is very delicate and vulnerable,' says Mike Figgis. 'He goes out on the wire sometimes for a character, leaving himself open for being hurt if something doesn't work. That's very rare. He has a range most actors would give their teeth for and he probably has a better intellectual background than most actors. Great acting is in proportion to intelligence.'

Cage's performances do not just happen, as Figgis discovered. In one sequence Ben has been in a fight in a bar and returns to Sera's apartment. He is angry but polite. Too polite, Figgis recalls: 'I was not quite prepared for him to say, "I feel like the kling-klang king of the rom-ram room", which wasn't in the script. So I shouted for the next take, "Good luck with the improvisation." Well, Nic got that look and said, "Oh, OK, I'll do a real straight one for ya, then." I had made the mistake of thinking it was arbitrary when, in fact, he'd worked it out very carefully. He's still very sensitive about the perception that he's wacky, because his performance isn't that. It was all hard work. Nothing in it was arbitrary.'

Cage reflects just how much change in his life resulted from *Leaving Las Vegas*: 'I was going through the thing with Kristen. I loved the person and although the relationship wasn't working I couldn't leave. I knew it wasn't right for me. I knew we were both unhappy. It was like we kept clinging to each other and it had to come to an end. So I went into therapy. I was loaded with all these feelings. Therapy was helpful and then I started thinking, Oh, man, they're taking all the good stuff from me. My acting had always been my therapy. The work was what saved me.'

Other help was at hand. During his couch sessions, he says, the face of Patricia Arquette kept flashing in his mind. After one session he went to the twenty-four-hour Jewish deli, Canter's, where they had met eight years earlier. It was two a.m. She was there. Happenstance? All Cage can remember is: 'She was wearing silver pants.' She remembers being impressed by 'his grandeur and his wildness and his sense of honour'.

Eight weeks later, she says, she was thinking about him and telephoned him and asked him to marry her. He said, 'Well, OK, I'll do it.'

She said: 'Well, goodbye, husband.'

He said: 'Wait! Can I get your phone number?'

Patricia Arquette was already considering what to wear on her wedding day.

There have been many versions of the events from the couple and

in 1997 they swore never to talk about their marriage again. They
wanted it 'protected like a species'. Once, when their situation was
described by someone as 'a Hollywood marriage', Arquette apparently
turned, like a Rottweiler, and spat, 'Don't you *ever* say that.'

Indeed, it was more than a Hollywood marriage could ever be.
Cage regards it as a historical union: 'I've always looked at it the way
they did in the old days when the father would say, "Your daughter
and my son are going to get married." They did. There was no
argument. And somehow those marriages lasted – often longer than
a lot of marriages last today. We love each other more than we ever
have. We've both been through enough to know that there are certain
responsibilities and certain elements of work that have to go into a
relationship. If the romance wears off there needs to be stability and
commitment – but I haven't felt any romance slipping away.'

How could he? Two weeks after Patricia Arquette's proposal on 6
April 1995, they were married on a Pacific clifftop outside the
Californian chocolate-box coastal resort of Carmel. The bride
remembers 'stormy skies, crashing waves, dark woods – and
everything out of focus except Nic in the centre with this light all
around him'. With the light were minister Kathee McFarland and her
husband, Donald, the town's former police chief. She officiated and
the two acted as witnesses. She remembers: 'He was real quiet. Patty
giggled a lot.'

Arquette wore a black vinyl suit and leopard-print jacket for the
ceremony, but more important to Cage was the wedding cake his
bride had brought: any fears he might have had vanished at the sight
of it. It was frosted in purple, his favourite colour.

'It was almost like an arranged marriage where we rushed into it.
We didn't have a natural courtship, we just did it. It was a romantic
gesture to marry as quickly as we did – but it was not a frivolous
decision,' Cage insists. 'I was genuinely aware of the work it takes to
make a marriage successful.'

'I was the one who proposed,' says Arquette. 'The second thing he
ever said to me was, "I'm going to marry you," and they say you end up
marrying somebody you lived five blocks from as a kid. We grew up
near each other in Hollywood. He'd asked me very often through the

years and at last I was ready. We both had kids of our own by then and neither of us had ever been married before. We're similar creatures.

'Marriage made me feel so exposed and raw. For the first time I wasn't putting protectors over myself. I was prying my ribs open and saying, "You're the one. I love you." It's an amazing feeling – really liberating.

'Girls come up to me and say, "It's *sooooooo* romantic," and that's true. It is *sooooo* romantic. It's like eight years ago we were both on the same train and we looked at each other and we knew, but we were immature. So he had to go run on top of the train and I went to go dance around in the diner car. And then we both got off the train at separate stops. And eight years later we both got back on and we sat next to each other and smiled. Suddenly, things didn't seem chaotic any more. I felt . . . what's the word? . . . *calm.*'

She wears a ring next to her gold wedding band from ancient Babylonia, the ring of Diana. Next to his wedding band he wears a gold ring with three coloured stones: one for Enzo, one for Weston and one for his wife.

Cage says: 'There was no question, no doubt in my mind that this woman was my equal and that I was meant to be with her from long ago. It never really left. I mean, we only went out for three weeks and went on with our lives and had these kind of extreme adventures exempt of one another that always somehow managed to keep us in synch, along with this parallel family connection in that she came from a creative family that would enact characters and skits and I can remember the exact same thing happening in my family with my brothers.

'We married each other. We're both from the same tribe, which is interesting to me. And I'm happy.

'I was ready to make that official commitment. I knew that it was time.'

He had met her in his 'bacchanalian era' and he married her in what was to be his 'Oscar time'. It's all so fantastically full of happenstance and coincidence. It was so Nicolas Cage. And, as it turns out, Mrs Cage. There was much more to *her* than purple-frosted wedding cake.

Chapter Seventeen

Mrs Cage

'It can be kind of like a freak show.' Patricia Arquette on being from an acting family.

Patricia Arquette and her husband indeed came from the same tribe: the acting one. She is a fourth-generation member of the performing Arquette family. Her great-grandparents were vaudevillians, her grandfather was the actor Cliff Arquette who, as 'Charley Weaver', was a regular on the long-running American game show *Hollywood Squares*. Her father, Lewis Arquette, was an actor on Broadway. Her sister Rosanna is an established, successful actress and played a New Jersey housewife in *Desperately Seeking Susan* while her brother Alexis played Lee Harvey Oswald in a Steppenwolf Theatre production of Don Delillo's *Libra*. He also has a nightclub act as the drag queen Eva Destruction. Her brother David was in *Wild Bill* with Jeff Bridges and Ellen Barkin – with whom he had a controversial affair before moving on to play a policeman in *Scream*. Her brother Richard is also an actor.

Their childhood reads like a parody of a 1960s upbringing. Both parents changed their names three times, as they veered from one spiritual quest to another. Eventually, their father converted to Islam. Their mother, Mardi (short for Mardiningshi), is Jewish, an ex-actress and part-time therapist. The couple are now separated.

The Arquette children were raised on a 'subud' commune in Virginia. (Subudism, says Lewis Arquette, is a 'non-sectarian fellowship', originating in Indonesia, that fosters meditation.) The Arquettes began performing early, in a children's version of *Paul Sills' Story Theatre*, and insist there is no competition among them. 'People expect friction,' says Rosanna. 'Leave us alone! I have my own work. I'm incredibly proud of Patricia. Because right now it is Patricia who is in the spotlight.'

A decade ago, however, Patricia was in full rebellion. During what she calls 'those troubled oestrogen-explosion periods I went from being an angel to a scathing, fire-breathing lunatic.' At twelve, she was arrested for shop-lifting. At fourteen, she shaved her head and ran away to live with Rosanna. At nineteen, she was pregnant by Paul Rossi. Their son Enzo became the fifth generation of Arquettes in the entertainment business when he played his mother's dead child in *Beyond Rangoon.*

When Patricia Arquette first began working, Hollywood was curious: everyone knew her sister and Arquette says, 'It can be kind of like a freak show, some kind of circus thing. First, when the industry hears of you they want to bring you in to see if you look like her, if you move like her, if you act like her. A lot of actors have a hard time getting seen, so in a way the family connection is a blessing but once you're in the door you're on your own. They either like *you* or they don't.'

She had never planned to go into the family business but in the end she couldn't resist. 'Rosanna took me on sets when I was twelve years old and I got to brag around school that I met Timothy Hutton. But I never thought I'd have the nerve to act.'

She was eighteen when she gave it a try with movies like *Pretty Smart* and *Nightmare on Elm Street 3: Dream Warriors.* A little more than a decade later she was one of the most sought-after leading ladies in the world. She got her first leading-lady role in *True Romance,* written by Quentin Tarantino and directed by Tony Scott. The British director is a fan: 'Patricia has all this darkness in her but also all this sweetness. It's rare to find that all rolled into one – usually you get looks or you get ability.'

True Romance was a landmark for all involved, especially Arquette and her co-star Christian Slater. Arquette was the newly minted hooker Alabama, all Spandex shorts and Day-glo push-up bra, and she had an important nude scene with Slater: 'We had to be totally naked. We did it close to the end of filming. We're sitting there naked with robes on. We throw them off and I grab his chin and hold it right there looking at him, blocking his eyes, and I say, "You better

just look at my eyes. Don't look at me. Swear you won't look at me."
And he goes, "Swear you won't look at me either." We were both
nervous and I was about to cry and he was about to cry and I think
that made the scene more tender. The truest wisdom is to approach
life like a child. Everybody has some weird hole that they have to have
filled.'

Arquette was magnificent with Liam Neeson in an adaptation of
Edith Wharton's *Ethan Frome*, and in Tim Burton's *Ed Wood*, in
which she played the understanding wife of the transvestite movie-
maker played by Johnny Depp. By 1997 she had completed John
Boorman's *Beyond Rangoon*, the quirky romantic comedy *Flirting
with Disaster*, with Ben Stiller, and an adaptation of Joseph Conrad's
Secret Agent, co-starring Bob Hoskins and Gerard Depardieu.

In the small world of Hollywood the connections were constant.
She was Sofia Coppola's lesbian lover in *Inside Monkey Zetterland*.
She had starred in *The Indian Runner* with Charles Bronson. Six years
later she was in *Nightwatch*, co-starring with Ewan *Trainspotting*
McGregor and Nick Nolte: a scary thriller about a serial killer
running loose in a morgue.

And in 1997 the world was seeing her in two roles in the same film,
Lost Highway. It was directed by David Lynch and took him back to
Wild at Heart country. Bill Pullman played jazz musician Fred
Madison, who may or may not have killed his wife Renee, played by
Arquette, who may or may not have been having an affair. The
parallel story involves Pete Dayton, played by Balthazar Getty, who is
lured into an affair with gangster's moll Alice, played by Arquette.
Now, this sexpot *femme fatale* may actually be Renee and Pete might
be Fred. Or they might not. As Cage's Sailor and Laura Dern's Lulu
had crisscrossed America, so these new and bizarre Lynch characters
puzzlingly screech through *Lost Highway*. One early review of the
film maintained that Arquette's 'carnal *oomph*' dominated the film.
Arquette smiles: 'It is a David Lynch film. It is not conventional.'

It is sexually explicit and features her in several nude scenes: 'I
trusted David not to be some hack about it. I have a real phobia about
nudity in my everyday life. I usually take a bath with the lights off. But
I wanted to confront this fear which I've fought my whole life so I was

gonna go through the gates of hell and see what it is.'

By *Lost Highway* her asking price was $2 million a film – not in the same league as her husband – and rising. Whenever film-makers want an immature/troubled/ sexually provocative woman she is the first call. Even as she approached thirty there was still a lot of Lolita about her. She is quick-witted and fey. The Malibu surfers call her 'chalk lady' because of her milky white skin which, with the bleached blonde hair and crooked front tooth, gives her an ephemeral quality that worked perfectly for the gum-popping hooker in *True Romance*, the loyal wife in *Ed Wood*, the servant-girl in *Ethan Frome*, the witless pregnant teenager in *Indian Runner*. Like a whole generation of actresses – Meg Ryan, Melanie Griffiths, Jennifer Jason Leigh – Arquette plays women who are sexual and at the same time childlike and unthreatening. She just does it better than most with frightening openness. 'Some women told me your uterus gets larger when you pass over the equator,' she says, laughing. 'I'm so gullible, I'm such a sucker that I believed them!'

In *Beyond Rangoon* she plays a doctor who travels to Burma on a voyage of self-discovery; she dyed her hair brown and was made to look as though she wasn't wearing any make-up. Boorman had seen her in *True Romance* and says: 'I was very impressed by her range, her unpredictable quality and a kind of boldness. When I met her I found a curious mixture of toughness and fragility.'

She may never be bland enough to make it in the commercial mainstream – but they said that of her fellow tribe member Nicolas Cage. As he says, they share remarkably similar backgrounds – although vastly different dynasties.

Arquette says that for many years she had been in search of 'an honourable, truthful, brave man'. Cage fitted the bill: 'He was on my mind and I needed to be reassured that the depth of his love would be as brave as before.'

Their first public appearance together as a married couple was at the Cannes Film Festival in 1995 when he was promoting *Kiss of Death* and she was discussing *Beyond Rangoon*. At one point Arquette was surrounded by half a dozen politely bowing members of the Japanese press corps. 'I'm on my honeymoon', she announced, lighting another Marlboro cigarette. Attempts to discuss the movie's message fell flat: the press wanted marital titbits. 'Do you have a lot of fun together?'

She looked lost, then replied: 'We stay home and talk a lot. Laugh a lot. Jump on the bed. Bark at each other.'

It was the turn of the Japanese writers to look lost.

'She has a cracked quality. Pure and impure at the same time,' said Tim Burton, who shares similar attributes.

At Cannes she was also asked: 'What is your relationship with sexuality?' She responded: 'I don't go around with a G-string and bullwhip. I guess I have a conflict about my sexuality and whether to be attractive or not, so I like playing around with it. You do a part like Alabama, who's all sexuality, and then you do a part like Laura in *Beyond Rangoon*, who's not. If you're going to like me as an actress, you're going to have to like me all the way.'

Sexual extremes have been a theme in Arquette's life and work. During the 'I hate men' phase after she broke up with Paul Rossi she would go to nightclubs in a tube dress and spiked heels and then berate 'the boys' for being attracted to her. Though she used to admire women like Isadora Duncan and Anaïs Nin, she says she sees them now as 'free-spirited but also with arrested development'. Her amended list of heroines includes Rosanna, her mother – 'both Marys from the Bible' – and Diane Keaton, who directed her in two TV films.

John Boorman had had a major problem with *Rangoon*. He explains: 'I had to find a major female star willing to spend six months in the jungle, fall in the mud, and get covered with leeches.' Not surprisingly, he says, Michelle Pfeiffer and Meryl Streep turned him down. Filming in Malaysia indeed proved demanding. Arquette spent much of her time running through jungle villages barefoot or up to her neck in brackish water. 'This movie should have been in "Smell-O-Vision". That river water smelled so bad. There'd be bloated dead kittens, human faeces.'

At Cannes, though, she was uneasy about how her performance would be received – especially by Cage. 'I wanted to put my hands over his eyes, but they have these spotlights that they shine on you in the theatre. I'm proud to be part of the movie, but I don't feel that good about my work in it.'

The Cage/Arquette marriage should not have come as any surprise: neither partner could ever be accused of playing the game of life by anyone else's rules. Both are renowned for their offbeat acting choices and a sense of personal style that defies all known aesthetic conventions. She likes to dress up as a cowgirl; he sports eccentric sideburns and head-to-toe black 'fashion'. She decorated her living room with prison art and old car-licence plates; he lived in a castle with turrets and a giant beetle laminated on the headboard of his bed.

Over the years Arquette had described her ideal man as 'someone who looked like Jesus but was kind of like a magician, a clown, and a pirate all mixed together' and someone confident enough to write 'his own moral code'. Cage has said he had 'always been attracted to crazy women' and 'wanted a woman who could really kick my ass'.

Before their marriage, Arquette asked her son what he thought of Cage: 'He's very honest. He would have said, "I don't like that guy." He didn't. I want to raise him and Weston with a liberal – and informed – attitude about everything. About the work Nic and I do.' About the nudity? The sex? 'Of course. I believe in love with sex. I've never had sex without love. I'll teach my kids that everybody wants to have sex, to see the naked body. I don't want them to feel bad about that but sex and love are best when you can have them together. I'll tell them, "Whatever you do with someone, make sure they want it equally or don't do it at all." And that you don't have to explain yourself to anybody. You're gay, straight, had a hundred lovers – who cares?

'I see the Bible as a code book to be a good person. Like Jesus loved Mary [Magdalene] so much. He wouldn't judge a woman on her sexual past. Who cares if she was a whore before he met her? It's not for you to decide whether somebody's past was right or wrong.'

Their marriage has taken the Tinseltown flak. There were stories that she had an affair with Ben Stiller while making *Flirting with Disaster* on location in Arizona in 1996. Cage was said to have been 'with' other women, including former flame Kristen. He says he and Zang became friends after his marriage: 'She was happy for me and my wife.' Cage nearly always refers to Arquette proudly as 'my wife'.

Arquette remarks that the gossip is all part of being a Hollywood couple: 'People are always looking at you when you're out. We don't go out a lot but if we do and we're in a crabby mood, people look at us and go: "Ooh, are there problems?" Friends call in the middle of the night because they've just read we're getting divorced. I pass the phone to Nicolas so they can hear we're still together. Sometimes, in the world we're in, what's sane seems insane.'

She says it was motherhood not marriage that changed her perception of men: 'Before my son, whatever man came along in my life was pivotal; however my career affected their security dictated what my career would be. I'm not there any more and haven't been in a long time.

'I know the marriage sounds really weird, incredibly abrupt, but we married out of a deep love for each other. Not out of sexuality. We hadn't slept together in eight years.

'You go through life trying to explain your moral code to whomever your partner is at the time. Half the time they think you're insane. But we are from the same tribe. We have the same moral code. There's no arguing about it.'

'I think she's a romantic', says her husband. 'There is a sense of mythology about her. I think she likes our story. I know I like it. It says of me that if I see something I want I go for it. I won't stop. I will not stop.'

Their friend Jim Carrey says: 'Their marriage was a very wild thing but I like them together. They're pretty cool and she's very cool. And you know I've been shocked by his devotion. He's really trying to make it work and be a good husband. And when Nic wants something to work . . .'

After he had won a clutch of awards for *Leaving Las Vegas* it was Oscar evening. Most stars are 'given' their gowns and jewels for the evening and the 'rocks' usually come from Harry Winston of Beverly Hills. Cage found his wife a little reticent about the glamour. 'She's the most anti-money person I know. I mean, I have a certain lifestyle and she's still trying to get comfortable with it. Not that she doesn't like the idea of objects and stuff, really. She went to Harry Winston's to get the diamonds all the girls were wearing and I said to her, "Honey, if I win this award the diamonds are yours." And the last thing she wants is diamonds – but I could tell she liked the idea and when I won, I said, "Well, we're both taking something home".

They did. And he moved on to an altogether different rock.

Chapter Eighteen
Rockets Galore

'I found him totally professional which is really something in this day and age.' Sean Connery, of his co-star in *The Rock*.

'**M**r Connery, I've got terrible news for you,' said the production assistant on the afternoon of Friday 19 January 1996. Sean Connery, who was literally knee-deep in making *The Rock*, was taken aback. His wife Micheline? His son Jason? What had happened?

'Mr Simpson's dead.'

Don Simpson, who with his partner Jerry Bruckheimer had made films like *Flashdance* (1983), *Beverly Hills Cop* (1984), *Top Gun* (1986) and *Crimson Tide* (1995), had been found on the floor of the upstairs bathroom of his Bel-Air home. His death had been caused by heart failure, brought on by a combination of cocaine and a dozen different sedatives, anti-depressants and anti-psychotics.

Connery said later, 'Having met him only once I was not completely surprised. He did not look well.'

Connery was playing the only man ever to escape from Alcatraz. His co-star was Cage, as a chemical weapons expert brought in to battle a band of terrorists who were threatening to launch a lethal gas attack on San Francisco from 'The Rock'. Simpson had been a major influence behind the $70-million action adventure. Bruckheimer decided to keep the news of his death from director Michael Bay until filming finished that Friday. Cage recalls: 'Somebody accidentally told me. It's difficult to concentrate when one of the conductors dies and you're still doing the piece.'

Michael Bay was trying to take Cage through a scene when he realized something wasn't working.

'Nic, what's going on?'

'Oh, I heard some bad news.'

'What are you talking about?'

'Don's dead.'

That's how Bay recalls the conversation: 'I sat down in my chair and freaked out. It was just tragic. We just shot that one shot and then I went into Jerry's trailer and I just sat there for a couple of hours.'

Cage's first venture into big budget action was as FBI agent Stanley Goodspeed, who had no field experience and was a somewhat geeky hero, but naïve or not, he has to dismantle the poison rockets held by Ed Harris's disgruntled military hero. It was all good *Boy's Own* stuff and Cage was an eager conscript: 'We all knew there was no character on the page at the beginning but I saw Stanley as a different kind of action hero, a reluctant one who is not heroic because he's got a steroid-ripped body or a robot head. I wanted to play a decent man who doesn't have an interest in killing and who doesn't swear.'

Neither he nor Connery nor Ed Harris were prepared for the rigours of filming on Alcatraz. 'The interior of the place is sinister and the weather is quick to change – it can be very cold, very warm. It's rather like Ireland in that you can get four seasons in one day.' Cage called the location Tetanus World but says: 'I felt silly complaining about it because I'm just an actor – there were guys who went through hell there.' He complained, though, about his dry suit, the protective clothing he had to wear for the Alcatraz invasion: 'I looked like Bubble Man. Sean looked so cool in his.'

It didn't help that the script was constantly rewritten. Connery had his writers and, before his death, Simpson would give 'notes' as would his partner. Cage remembers: 'There were a lot of cooks in the kitchen. Jerry Bruckheimer is very similar to my uncle Francis in that way. Things are always being changed, being tweaked.' Earlier he had said: 'The fact of the matter is I rewrote most of my dialogue. It just wasn't on the page. I can come up with melodies and rhythms that I've always explored – it's a stylistic thing.' This upset the film's various writers, although they admit that he introduced aspects of his character, including Stanley's obsessions with Beatles songs. Cage even changed his character's name from Bill to Stanley, explaining:

'My dentist is Stanley Golden and his manner is interesting and some of it was right for the role.' David Weisberg and Douglas Cook, who were credited with the screenplay, were irritated by everyone else taking kudos for their work. Weisberg said: 'Nic Cage, Sean Connery, Michael Bay and Jerry Bruckheimer would not have been there if it had not been for our writing the dialogue and creating the characters. For Nic Cage to look at a line he rewrote and take responsibility is insulting. It remains ours – the characters, the story, the action are the same as we wrote.'

Whoever was ultimately responsible, it was a challenge for Cage – and fun: 'It was probably the most expensive movie I had ever made but for some reason I got that Super-8 feeling I had when I was a kid and my brother and I used to make movies. It was like, "OK, now you're gonna fall down – then you pick the gun up." Ironically, the bigger the movie and the more action, the more it feels like playing in the back yard. That fun is an infectious feeling. As long as you come from that good place where you know you're enjoying yourself then I think the movie works – a movie like *The Rock*, where the idea is fun and escape and adventure are seminal to the process.'

In 1963 Alcatraz was closed because its foundations were decaying but it became a tourist attraction with more than 1.5 million visitors every year. Michael Bay decided they had to film on location, which meant much organization. Cage says: 'It was an intense shoot. There were some safety measures that had to be constantly observed. In one scene Sean and I had to be underwater while a ball of flame "rolled" over us.'

For Connery it was an excuse to bait the director: 'If I screw up, my hair is going to burn off, is that right? Why don't you try it?'

Technical adviser, and Connery's safety driver, Harry Humphries recalls: 'He was sixty-five years old then and he did the job. My only concern was that he would pop up and panic but he did not.' The idea of Connery panicking is hard to swallow.

It was difficult, at first, for Cage to work with a man whose career he had followed all his life – he can recite lines from *Dr No* – but an exceptional degree of mutual respect grew between the two actors – and Connery has never suffered fools and usually only endorses cheques.

Cage kept him enthusiastic about *The Rock* and Connery says of his co-star: 'I found him totally professional, which is really something in this day and age. We got on well.'

Cage saw it this way: 'He became to some extent a mentor to me, which is a difficult relationship for actors to find. He likes actors and he doesn't like to be bullshitted or double-crossed. He validated some of my thoughts that I was concerned about. He's enjoying a career where he's at the top of his form at his age which is remarkable. I mean, who gets to act that long and still be the event with every movie? I would ask him questions about determining image – you know the movie star image. What about an actor who wants to change his voice or his look? He said, "Don't worry about that, don't concern yourself with image. Just do your work."'

There were echoes of that in some lines from *The Rock*. Just before going into action against Ed Harris and his terrorists, Stanley assures Connery as John Mason, 'I'll do my best.' Mason turns around angrily and says: 'Losers always whine about their best. Winners go home and fuck the Prom Queen.'

That line hit home.

Chapter Nineteen

Action Man

I'm sure I'm going to make movies that are going to piss people off.' Nicolas Cage on his post-Oscar career.

The combination of Cage and Connery made *The Rock* one of the box-office successes of 1996. But Cage then turned down the chance to work again with Mike Figgis, believing that the director's delve into infidelity in marriage was a little too soon after his own marriage. 'I was not in a place in my world at that time, right after I'd gotten married, where I wanted to play a man who was cheating on his wife. It just wasn't somewhere I wanted to go. I just didn't want to go there.'

Instead he went to work with some major stars in two action films, both of which were released in the summer of 1997. He joined up for the Jerry-Bruckheimer-produced *Con-Air*, which tells the story of Cameron Poe, who is jailed for murdering in self-defence but then paroled. He is desperate to be with the daughter he has never seen and hitches a lift on a federal government transport plane, part of the Con-Air fleet. Also on board is John Malkovich as Cyrus 'The Virus' Grissom – a bad guy with an appetite like Hannibal 'The Cannibal' Lecter of Silence of the Lambs – who has meticulously planned a mid-air hijacking. On the ground is John Cusack as US Marshall Vince Larkin, who must team up with Poe to stop the convicts going on a killing spree and the authorities from blasting the transporter out of the sky as it heads for the Las Vegas Strip. As Cage would say: 'The casino is open.' The gambling began before filming when he visited California's Folsom State Prison to do research: 'I had to sign an acknowledgement that said that there was a no hostage-policy at the jail, which meant that if I was taken hostage – too bad. I couldn't sue. So I go out in the yard with three thousand killers. My adrenaline was really high. I wanted to interview some of the guys who I thought would look like my character. It was scary. I asked one guy, "How do you stay alive?" He said, "You just got to get hectic." I said, "What do you mean?" He said, "Just got to get desperate, man." There was one guy with four tattooed tears down one side of his face, a moustache, a shaved head and a Jewish star on the other side of his face. I went up to this big white guy who wore these wraparound shades and said, "Listen, hi, I'm making a movie and I'm just an actor but is there anything about jail life that you'd like to see in a movie that you haven't seen, anything about movies that deal with prison that really pisses you off?" He just stared at me and said, "I got nothing to say to you." I left.'

Cage found humour in working with Malkovich: 'I had to laugh at one moment because here's John Malkovich, one of the most revered actors of stage and film for the last twenty years, and I finally get to work with him and what we are doing is standing on top of a fire truck and he's coming at me with an axe and I'm hitting him with a pole. 'I thought, I guess we're not doing Steinbeck or Eugene O'Neill. We're going to be kids again, aren't we?'

But even that was not simple. There was some opposition from the producers to his Southern blue collar definition of Cameron Poe: 'They said I wasn't being "Nic Cage". They got over it but it takes time for a character to get up and running.' And he *is* a character. He'd insisted on showing his pumped-up body during *The Rock* – when he is seen in his apartment strumming a guitar wearing just pink-purple underpants – despite his good shape going against Stanley's nerdy character. And he strutted his stuff in *Con-Air*. 'There are plenty of scenes of him stripped to the waist taking care of business,' said director Simon West.

Even more high profile was *Face Off*, which teamed Cage with John Travolta. They are terrorist and cop whose faces are switched scientifically, which means that Cage plays Travolta and vice versa.

Director John Woo, who guided Travolta in *Broken Arrow*, hired Travolta first, who explained: 'It's kind of a mix between action, sci-fi and drama. It's set in the future – not too much in the future, about twenty years from now, and there's an ability to change faces. Through a series of events we change so I play Nic and he plays me two or three different times. Nic and I had to figure out how to play, what choices to make. It was a very interesting puzzle to solve. John Woo and I were in from the start and we went to Nic. We really wanted him to join in. I'm so happy he did.'

Cage was honoured at the Montreal World Film Festival in September 1996, the youngest person ever to receive their Lifetime Achievement Award. He was thirty three. 'It had tremendous meaning for me – the recognition of fifteen years of work that had often met with opposition. It's hard for an actor to have the purity of expression if he is perceived as being different. There were days when I was told I would never work again. So I was encouraged to stay true to myself . . . '

Staying true did not slow him down. In 1998 he is planning *Speed Racer*, based on the 1967 cartoon series of the same title. Maverick Gus Van Sant is in line to direct. There is also talk of a sequel to his 1983 *Valley Girl*, which seems such a long time ago. He rather liked the nostalgia idea. But there were lots of others tumbling about his mind.

He is keen to work with Quentin Tarantino, whom he met at an awards tribute to Clint Eastwood. Cage says: 'He told me it would be really cool if I screamed out "fuck" at the Academy Awards ceremony if I lost. I told him what he needed to do to be cool right there and then. Everybody was at the dinner – Jack Nicholson, Dustin Hoffman, Warren Beatty; "even Don Rickles" I said. "I know a way you can be really cool. If you want to be really cool stand up right now and yell that you're the biggest star in the room. Just do that and you'll be really cool." He started laughing, like, "Don't make me do that." But he's a great director – his movies have a whole new energy. It's like certain kinds of music that I listen to – uncompromising, angry music. It comes out as sort of an assault.'

Of course, in his bad-boy days Cage would have been doing the jumping up and down, probably Elvis style, in line with his 'just do it' motto.

Now, it was more cool to be cool. And there were the responsibilities of the superstar millions he was being paid.

He also wants to work with his wife. The couple are keen to take on the legendary roles of Nick and Nora Charles, the martini-loving detectives brought to life by William Powell and Myrna Loy in *The Thin Man*, which also starred Jimmy Stewart. Arquette says: 'We've done heavy movies – now it's time to have fun.' Which her husband has always been good at doing. But now he has emerged as a superstar he is getting roles to match his status. Like playing an angel – for $12 million.

In April 1997, Cage began filming *City of Angels* – a freewheeling update of director Wim Wenders's *Wings of Desire* – with Meg Ryan. In a departure from his Dracula-loving days he plays a guardian angel who falls in love with the woman he's assigned to watch over. The movie aims to reflect Los Angeles – the city of Angels – in all its multicultural complexities and absurdities.

He was also in talks to co-star with Will Smith from *Independence Day* for Brian DePalma – hot following the financial success of *Mission Impossible* – in *Snake Eyes*. Cage would play a detective who witnesses the assassination of the US Secretary of Defense during a heavyweight boxing title fight – and must find the killer before the fight is over.

Most appropriate of all for Cage was the offer to take on the dual personality of the movies' best loved hero – Superman. Producer Jon Peters wanted Cage to take on the role of Superman/Clark Kent in *Superman Reborn* which Warner Brothers aimed to have in cinemas worldwide by the summer of 1998. It's a bird! It's a plane! It's Nicolas Cage? With this maverick of the movies no feat, it seems, is impossible. Sandra Bullock is set to co-star as Lois Lane in the new adventure of the Man of Steel.

In 1997 in the Superman comics, which mirror his film and television persona, our hero spurned his traditional look – and cape – when he became 'an electrical being'. His primary school red and yellow 'S' logo was stylized for the 1990s and, most importantly, his crimson Y-fronts were replaced by an electric blue and white all-in-one bodysuit. Comic book fans were not impressed. It appeared that the comic book Superman would return to his former style but retain his new powers.

And what of Clark Kent who Lois called 'an unbearable coward' in the first comic book story more than half a century ago? With Nic Cage in charge he will surely develop a more expressive nervous tic than adjusting his spectacles with one finger whenever his superhearing tunes into trouble. With a pumped up mind *and* pectorals, mixed in with a wild imagination, the expectations are of a very intriguing turn-of-the-century Superman. To go with his super-life?

'I'm really happy with my life but I also know everything can be transitory. Life is always full of surprises and I'm not just going to let myself get lazy and say it's always going to be this way . . .'

Epilogue

Surf's Up

'I've become the black sheep of my family.' Nicolas Cage, 1997.

D espite his success in both his career and his personal life, Nicolas Cage still has his problems. There are frustrations over his shared custody of his son, and his own estrangement from his father over remarks they both probably regret. 'My family is passionate, competitive and crazy,' Cage says. 'There's a very strange male dynamic in my family and I don't know where it comes from but it's there. There's a tremendous amount of jealousy and competition in my family. For a family that is portrayed as close-knit there's an awful lot of that Old Country jealousy and that sort of stuff and I try to distance myself from it and I don't want to be part of it. I'm sure that's been going on for hundreds of years in Naples or somewhere but I don't particularly feel comfortable in it and so I try not play that. In some ways I've become the black sheep of my family. There's a distance that's happened which I think is very frustrating and I don't think it comes from love. I think it comes from the want to control and I don't want to be controlled.'

What he did want to get into more in 1997 was surfing. He and Arquette paid $3.5 million for a five-bedroom Cape-Cod-style home in Malibu. The gated estate on an acre of land right on the Pacific has a cobblestone drive, its own creek and a swimming pool. It is for family surfing at weekends and days off.

He says he will never write an autobiography. But if he did what would be the title? Instantly he replies: '*Back Off, There's a Lobster Loose.*'

What would be the byline? Nicolas Cage? Nicolas Coppola?

'I've become who I am now and that's Cage. Nicolas Coppola is not around any more.'

But is it the Nicolas Cage who has wooed Hollywood and moviegoers with his often wild and way out performances? Has he, as many critics want to believe, mellowed? Definitely not. The casino remains open.

Sure, as he says, he may 'piss off' fans with the films he makes but the eccentricity that made him a star marches on to a very different drummer than the rest of ego-and-money inflated Hollywood. Yes, he has moved out to surf country, but it involves more than just catching some waves.

What of Dracula's domain, the castle in the Hollywood Hills? He is thinking of having it torn down – and rebuilt with stone imported from Britain. It would seem an expensive venture. He explains: 'I just don't like stucco. I want some authentic stone from dilapidated English castles. I don't like that prefab cottage cheese spray-on crap and my house has that now unfortunately. I've tried to sandblast it off. I've tried to put a night-growing creeper around it. And nothing works. So it's just time to bring over a castle and start over . . . '

Nicolas Cage retains the crown.

UNCAGED

The filmography of

NICOLAS CAGE

Fast Times at Ridgemont High, 1982, Universal Pictures.
  Starring: **Nicolas Coppola** with **Sean Penn** and **Judge Reinhold**.
  Director: **Amy Heckerling**.

Rumble Fish, 1983, Universal Pictures.
  Starring: **Nicolas Coppola** with **Matt Dillon**, **Mickey Rourke** and **Christopher Penn**.
  Director: **Francis Ford Coppola**.

Valley Girl, 1983, Atlantic Releasing Corporation.
  Starring: **Nicolas Cage** with **Deborah Foreman**, **Elizabeth Daily** and
  Michael Bowen.
  Director: **Martha Coolidge**.

Racing With the Moon, 1984, Paramount Pictures.
  Starring: **Sean Penn, Elizabeth McGovern, Nicolas Cage**.
  Director: **Richard Benjamin**.

The Cotton Club, 1984, Zeotrope/Orion Pictures.
  Starring: **Richard Gere, Gregory Hines, Bob Hoskins, Diane Lane, Nicolas Cage**.
  Director: **Francis Ford Coppola**.

Birdy, 1985, TriStar Pictures.
  Starring: **Matthew Modine, Nicolas Cage**.
  Director: **Alan Parker**.

The Boy in Blue, 1986, Canadian Co-op Productions.
  Starring: **Nicolas Cage, Christopher Plummer, David Naughton**.
  Director: **Charles Jarrott**.

Peggy Sue Got Married, 1986, TriStar Pictures.
  Starring: **Kathleen Turner, Nicolas Cage, Crispin Glover, Jim Carrey**.
  Director: **Francis Ford Coppola**.

Raising Arizona, 1987, Orion Pictures.
>> Starring: **Nicolas Cage, Holly Hunter, John Goodman**.
>> DIrector: **Joel Coen**.

Moonstruck, 1987, Universal Pictures.
>> Starring: **Cher, Nicolas Cage, Olympia Dukakis, Danny Aiello**.
>> Director: **Norman Jewison**.

Vampire's Kiss, 1989, ICI Independent.
>> Starring: **Nicolas Cage, Jennifer Beals, Maria Conchita Alonso**.
>> Director: **Robert Bierman**.

Fire Birds, 1990, Arnold Kopelson Productions.
>> Starring: **Nicolas Cage, Sean Young, Tommy Lee Jones**.
>> Director: **David Green**.

Wild at Heart, 1990, Orion Pictures.
>> Starring: **Nicolas Cage, Laura Dern, Diane Ladd, Harry Dean Stanton, Willem Dafoe, Isabella Rossellini**.
>> Director: **David Lynch**.

Zandalee, 1991, Independent Pictures.
>> Starring: **Nicolas Cage, Judge Reinhold, Erika Anderson**.
>> Director: **Sam Pillsbury**.

Honeymoon in Vegas, 1992, Castlerock Entertainment.
>> Starring: **Nicolas Cage, Sarah Jessica Parker, James Caan, Anne Bancroft**.
>> Director: **Andrew Bergman**.

Amos and Andrew, 1993, Castlerock Entertainment.
>> Starring: **Nicolas Cage, Samuel L. Jackson**.
>> Directoɾ: **E. Max Frye**.

Deadfall, 1993, Independent.
>> Starring: **Nicolas Cage**.
>> Director: **Christopher Coppola**.

Guarding Tess, 1994, TriStar Pictures.
>> Starring: **Nicolas Cage, Shirley MacLaine**.
>> Director: **Hugh Wilson**.

It Could Happen To You, 1994,Castlerock Entertainment.
>> Starring: **Nicolas Cage, Bridget Fonda, Rosie Perez**.
>> Director: **Andrew Bergman**.

Red Rock West, 1994, Propaganda Films.
>> Starring: **Nicolas Cage, Lara Flynn Boyle, Dennis Hopper**.
>> Director: **John Dahl**.

Trapped in Paradise, 1994, Universal Pictures.
>> Starring: **Nicolas Cage, Dana Carvey** and **Jon Lovitz**.
>> Director: **Andrew Jordan**.

Kiss of Death, 1995, TriStar Pictures.
>> Starring: **Nicolas Cage, David Caruso**.
>> Director: **Barbet Schroeder**.

Leaving Las Vegas, 1995, MGM.
>> Starring: **Nicolas Cage, Elisabeth Shue**.
>> Director: **Mike Figgis**.

The Rock, 1996, Simpson-Bruckheimer/ Hollywood Pictures.
>> Starring: **Nicolas Cage, Sean Connery, Ed Harris**.
>> Director: **Michael Bay**.

Con-Air, 1997, Bruckheimer Productions/ Hollywood Pictures.
>> Starring: **Nicolas Cage, John Malkovich, John Cusack, Steve Buscemi, Ving Rhames, Rachel Ticotin**.
>> Director: **Simon West**.

Face Off, 1997, Warner Brothers.
>> Starring: **Nicolas Cage, John Travolta**.
>> Director: **John Woo**.

In development:

Speed Racer, 1998, Donner/Schuler Donner Productions/ Silver Pictures/ Warner Brothers.
>> Starring: **Nicolas Cage, Johnny Depp**.
>> Director: **Gus Van Sant**.

Valley Girl 2, 1998, Motion Picture Corporation of America (MPCA).
>> Starring: **Nicolas Cage**.
>> Director: **Troy Beyer-Burg**.

UNCAGED

The Index